FORTRESS • 102

DEFENSE OF THE RHINE 1944–45

STEVEN J ZALOGA

ILLUSTRATED BY ADAM HOOK

Series editor Marcus Cowper

First published in 2011 by Osprey Publishing
Midland House, West Way, Botley, Oxford OX2 0PH, UK
44-02 23rd St, Suite 219, Long Island City, NY 11101, USA

E-mail: info@ospreypublishing.com

A CIP catalog record for this book is available from the British Library.

ISBN: 978 1 84908 387 4
E-book ISBN: 978 1 84908 388 1

Editorial by Ilios Publishing Ltd, Oxford, UK (www.iliospublishing.com)
Cartography by Bounford
Page layout by Ken Vail Graphic Design, Cambridge, UK (kvgd.com)
Typeset in Myriad and Sabon
Index by Alison Worthington
Originated by United Graphics Pte
Printed in in China through Bookbuilders

11 12 13 14 15   10 9 8 7 6 5 4 3 2 1

Osprey Publishing are supporting the Woodland Trust, the UK's leading woodland conservation charity, by funding the dedication of trees.

www.ospreypublishing.com

AUTHOR'S NOTE

The author would like to thank Neil Short for the use of photographs in this book. The photographs here come primarily from the US National Archives and Records Administration (NARA) at College Park, MD, and from the Library and Archives Canada (LAC).

For brevity, the traditional conventions have been used when referring to units. In the case of US units, 1/179th Infantry refers to the 1st Battalion, 179th Infantry Regiment. The US Army traditionally uses Arabic numerals for divisions and smaller independent formations (70th Division, 781st Tank Battalion), Roman numerals for corps (VI Corps), spelled-out numbers for field armies (Seventh Army) and Arabic numerals for army groups (12th Army Group).

In the case of German units, 2./Panzer-Regiment 7 refers to the 2nd Company, Panzer-Regiment 7; II./Panzer-Regiment 7 indicates 2nd Battalion, Panzer-Regiment 7. German corps have two accepted forms, the formal version using Roman numerals (LXXXIV Armee Korps) or the shortened 84. AK which is the preferred form used here for clarity. Likewise, the German field armies are contracted in the usual fashion (e.g. AOK 19 for Nineteenth Army).

ARTIST'S NOTE

THE FORTRESS STUDY GROUP (FSG)

The object of the FSG is to advance the education of the public in the study of all aspects of fortifications and their armaments, especially works constructed to mount or resist artillery. The FSG holds an annual conference in September over a long weekend with visits and evening lectures, an annual tour abroad lasting about eight days, and an annual Members' Day.

The FSG journal *FORT* is published annually, and its newsletter *Casemate* is published three times a year. Membership is international. For further details, please contact:

secretary@fsgfort.com
Website: www.fsgfort.com

THE HISTORY OF FORTIFICATION STUDY CENTER (HFSC)

The History of Fortification Study Center (HFSC) is an international scientific research organization that aims to unite specialists in the history of military architecture from antiquity to the 20th century (including historians, art historians, archeologists, architects and those with a military background). The center has its own scientific council, which is made up of authoritative experts who have made an important contribution to the study of fortification.

The HFSC's activities involve organizing conferences, launching research expeditions to study monuments of defensive architecture, contributing to the preservation of such monuments, arranging lectures and special courses in the history of fortification and producing published works such as the refereed academic journal *Questions of the History of Fortification*, monographs and books on the history of fortification. It also holds a competition for the best publication of the year devoted to the history of fortification.

The headquarters of the HFSC is in Moscow, Russia, but the center is active in the international arena and both scholars and amateurs from all countries are welcome to join. More detailed information about the HFSC and its activities can be found on the website: www.hfsc.3dn.ru

E-mail: ciif-info@yandex.ru

CONTENTS

DEFENSE OF THE RHINE 1944–45

INTRODUCTION

The Rhine has been Germany's traditional defensive barrier in the west since Roman times. In the autumn and early winter of 1944–45, the Wehrmacht conducted an extensive fortification effort in the foreground of the Rhine, consisting of the rejuvenation of the derelict Westwall fortifications, the incorporation of parts of the Maginot Line, and the construction of numerous new defensive lines. This was known as the West-Stellung (West Position).

This defense system has been surrounded by confusion and obscurity. It is often confused with the Westwall, the German fortification effort of 1936–40. While large parts of the Westwall were incorporated into the new fortification scheme, the new defensive lines covered areas not previously reached by the Westwall, and considerably amplified the depth of the defenses. Another source of confusion is the nickname "Siegfried Line," which has been loosely used over the years to refer both to the 1940 Westwall as well as the far more extensive defenses of 1944–45. The Siegfried Line misnomer stemmed from Hitler's April 28, 1939 Reichstag speech in which he described the new Westwall as 40 times stronger than the old Siegfried-Stellung fieldworks of 1918. Due to a misunderstanding, the British press began referring to the Westwall fortifications as the Siegfried Line in 1939–40. When Allied forces

This bucolic view shows a stretch of the West-Stellung in the Wissembourg Gap near Steinfeld in March 1945. In the foreground are freshly dug trench lines while in the background are a number of Westwall bunkers and the ubiquitous fields of dragon's teeth. (NARA)

4

West-Stellung, February 1945

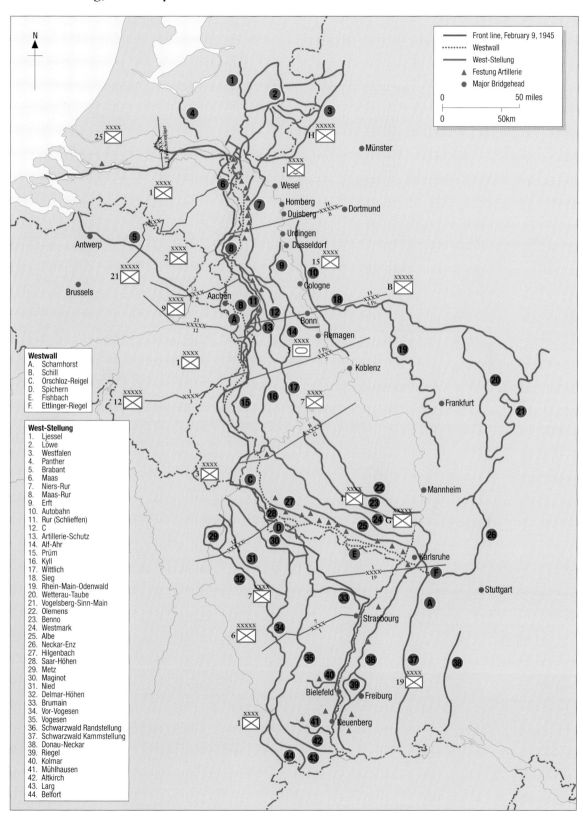

Legend:
- Front line, February 9, 1945
- Westwall
- West-Stellung
- ▲ Festung Artillerie
- ● Major Bridgehead

0 — 50 miles
0 — 50km

Westwall
A. Scharnhorst
B. Schill
C. Orschloz-Reigel
D. Spichern
E. Fishbach
F. Ettlinger-Riegel

West-Stellung
1. Ljessel
2. Löwe
3. Westfalen
4. Panther
5. Brabant
6. Maas
7. Niers-Rur
8. Maas-Rur
9. Erft
10. Autobahn
11. Rur (Schlieffen)
12. C
13. Artillerie-Schutz
14. Alf-Ahr
15. Prüm
16. Kyll
17. Wittlich
18. Sieg
19. Rhein-Main-Odenwald
20. Wetterau-Taube
21. Vogelsberg-Sinn-Main
22. Olemens
23. Benno
24. Westmark
25. Albe
26. Neckar-Enz
27. Hilgenbach
28. Saar-Höhen
29. Metz
30. Maginot
31. Nied
32. Delmar-Höhen
33. Brumain
34. Vor-Vogesen
35. Vogesen
36. Schwarzwald Randstellung
37. Schwarzwald Kammstellung
38. Donau-Neckar
39. Riegel
40. Kolmar
41. Mühlhausen
42. Altkirch
43. Larg
44. Belfort

Münster · Wesel · Homberg · Duisberg · Dortmund · Urdingen · Dusseldorf · Cologne · Bonn · Remagen · Koblenz · Frankfurt · Mannheim · Karlsruhe · Stuttgart · Strasbourg · Bielefeld · Freiburg · Neuenberg · Antwerp · Brussels · Aachen

reached the old Westwall in September 1944, the German defensive positions were again called the Siegfried Line.

Hitler summed up the intention of the West-Stellung in a September 1944 directive, which stated:

> In the West, the fighting has advanced onto German soil along broad sectors. German cities and villages are becoming part of the combat zone. This fact must make us fight with fanatical determination and put up stiff resistance with every able-bodied man in the combat zone. Each pillbox, every city and village block must become a fortress against which the enemy will smash himself to bits or in which the German garrison will die in hand-to-hand fighting. There can be no large-scale operations on our part any longer. All we can do is hold our positions or die.

The 1944–45 West-Stellung program differed considerably from the earlier Westwall. Due to the poor weather, as well as the lack of material and skilled labor, few new concrete bunkers were constructed. The old Westwall served as the concrete spine of the new West-Stellung and additional defensive lines were layered around it using fieldworks reinforced with obstacles and gun emplacements. Special emphasis was placed on antitank defense in the form of numerous antitank obstacles as well as dense antitank-gun positions. Instead of a thin and brittle string of obsolete concrete bunkers, the West-Stellung offered defense in depth. Construction of the West-Stellung was mainly carried out by labor drafts from the cities along the Rhine. It was an enormous civic undertaking, exceeding 400,000 laborers by October 1944.

The West-Stellung was a significant enhancement to the Wehrmacht campaign in the west in the autumn of 1944, serving both to reinforce the declining combat effectiveness of German infantry units while at the same time providing a shield behind which the Army could hoard its elite Panzer units for the planned December offensive in the Ardennes. The West-Stellung proved far less effective in February–March 1945 when the Allies began their final offensive to the Rhine. No fortification system could compensate for the crippling losses suffered in the failed Ardennes campaign, and the new defensive lines were quickly overwhelmed by the Allied onslaught. A further defense scheme on the east bank of the Rhine, the Rhein-Stellung, was largely stillborn and was overrun before completion in March–April 1945. This book is the first comprehensive description in English of the 1944–45 West-Stellung fortification program.

DESIGN AND DEVELOPMENT

The Westwall legacy

Adolf Hitler had been the driving force behind the Third Reich's previous fortification efforts, the Westwall along the French border in 1938–39 and the Atlantic Wall (Atlantikwall) in 1942–44. The Westwall was a pale imitation of the neighboring French Maginot Line, consuming less than 4 million cubic meters of concrete compared to over 12 million for the French program. The Westwall was as much a strategic political bluff as a genuine defensive line. Hitler created a propaganda image of an impregnable fortress to intimidate the French Army and give the Wehrmacht a free hand in Czechoslovakia and Poland in 1938–39. After the defeat of France in 1940 its mission had been accomplished, so the Westwall was largely abandoned.

The pre-war Westwall served as the concrete spine of the new West-Stellung. This is a typical stretch of the Westwall with rows of dragon's teeth in the foreground covered by an armored machine-gun cupola. These armored cupolas were the only visible portion of a much more extensive bunker underneath. This particular example is a 40P8 Sechsschartenturm, a widely used cupola type armored to A1 standards. (NARA)

The Westwall was heavily based on relatively small infantry bunkers with machine-gun armament but few of the massive artillery bunkers that were so characteristic of the great French "ouvrages" of the Maginot Line. The Westwall began along the German frontier with a barrier of antitank ditches and dragon's teeth antitank obstacles. The layout and density of the subsequent bunkers depended on the local geography and was designed to exploit local terrain features. Machine-gun bunkers were placed to cover all key roads and approaches as well as to prevent the antitank obstacles from being breached. Antitank bunkers armed with 37mm and 47mm antitank guns covered the antitank traps. Forward observation posts for artillery spotters were connected to the rear to take maximum advantage of artillery firepower in defending the frontier.

Behind the main line of resistance were larger bunker complexes, nicknamed *B-Werke* or *B-Stellung* as they were protected to the medium "B" standard of protection (*Mittlerer Ausbaustärke B*). This standard translated to walls of 2m-thick steel-reinforced concrete, which could withstand direct artillery fire from 220mm guns or 500kg bombs. The smaller machine-gun bunkers were mostly built to the B1 construction standard, which had walls 1.5m thick designed to protect against 155mm guns. About 85 percent of the Westwall fortifications were built to B1 standard, and 11 percent to B standard. The higher A standard, with walls 3.5m thick, was reserved mainly for artillery observation bunkers and constituted about 2 percent of the total. The total number of bunkers completed by 1940 was about 17,755 across 530 miles (850km) of frontier.

An example of a very simple MG-Schartenstand built to B1 standards in the Aachen area as part of the original Westwall. These would contain a single machine gun, often an old MG 08 from World War I. (NARA)

By 1944 standards, the Westwall was out of date and in serious need of rejuvenation. Its minefields had been lifted and most of the barbed-wire entanglements removed. With the acceleration of the Atlantikwall program in 1943, anything that could be easily removed from the Westwall was cannibalized to help in the anti-invasion effort. Armored doors and internal fittings were recycled and the Westwall became little more than a concrete shell. The iconic rows of dragon's teeth were intact, though in some sectors local farmers had pushed earth over them in order to create access ways so they could move

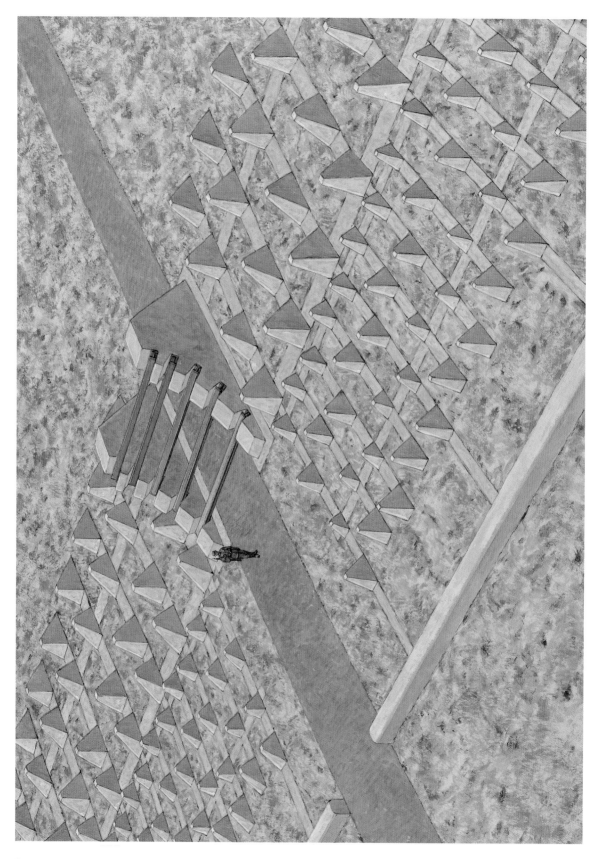

Most major bridges along the major western waterways were fortified during the 1936–40 Westwall program. This is a *Brückensicherungsbunker* (bridge security bunker) on the Saar near Dillingen, part of the heavily reinforced Saarpfalz defense sector. (NARA)

around their property. The nominal table of organization for the Westwall was a garrison of about 200,000 troops, but by mid-1943 there were only 15,715 men assigned to the fortifications, in most cases local militia or training units. In 1943 the Army proposed rejuvenating the Westwall in the event that the anticipated Allied invasion succeeded. A plan codenamed "Sunshine" (Sonne) was proposed to resurrect the fortification lines, but Hitler refused to divert resources from his favored Atlantikwall effort.

The only significant fortification effort in 1943 was the extension of the Westwall into the Netherlands as the Holland-Stellung. The Westwall covered only the southern end of the Dutch border, and there was some concern that the Dutch rivers offered a convenient access route into Germany's industrial heartland in the Ruhr. On September 15, 1943 the Oberkommando des Heeres (OKH) ordered the creation of the new Lower Rhine Fortification Command, or Kommandantur der Befestigungen Niederrhein (KBN), under Generalleutnant Walter Eckstein, in order to develop a suitable barrier. Since the Westwall largely ended at Kleve, the immediate task was to add a Westwall extension northward from Westervoort towards Groningen and the Frisian coast on the North Sea. Additional sectors were added to the KBN program late in 1943, including an extension from Nijmegen to Roermond, sometimes called the Neue HKL (New Main Line of Resistance). Since resources were

A DRAGON'S TEETH ANTITANK OBSTACLE

Among the most characteristic and enduring legacies of the original Westwall program were the fields of dragon's teeth, known officially in German as *Eisenbetonhöckerhindernisse* (steel-reinforced protruding obstructions). These were generally emplaced as connected fields of obstructions, not as individual obstacles, and they had a distinctive pattern of lower obstacles followed by higher obstacles in order to encourage enemy tanks to attempt to surmount the low obstacles at the edge of the field, which would cause them to become stuck on the higher obstacles deeper in the field. Some fields began with a wall at the beginning. The actual size and shape of the obstacles changed with time, with the smaller and lower obstacles being the Typ 1938 (alter Art) and the larger and angled examples in

the second row being the Typ 1939 (neuer Art). These fields were sometimes reinforced through the course of Westwall construction, hence the mixture of types. To provide access through the fields, special road blockades (Straßensperre) were developed, which could be left open in peacetime and then closed off in the event of combat. This particular type used steel "I" beams, which were stored next to the obstacle in peacetime and then placed into the slots in the concrete obstacle when needed. There were steel attachment points inside the slot to attach the beams solidly in place. These fields of dragon's teeth were not expected to stop a tank advance on their own, but would be covered by nearby antitank guns either in bunkers or fieldworks.

One of the earliest efforts to shield the Rhine took place in 1943, carried out by the Kommandantur der Befestigungen Neiderrhein in the Netherlands to cover the area north of the pre-war fortification efforts with a Westwall extension. Here, in 1945, Canadian troops of B Company, Highland Light Infantry, examine a row of dragon's teeth erected near the Afsluitdijk causeway that seals off the Ijsselmeer from the North Sea in the northern Netherlands. (LAC PA-133282)

limited, the engineers used the canals in the region as the basis for a defensive line. Little concrete or steel reinforcing bar was available for permanent bunkers, so the effort concentrated mainly on the construction of temporary fieldworks near major towns and canal crossing points.

Fortification in the foreground of the Rhine

Prior to the Normandy invasion, there was some discussion about creating a Zweite-Stellung (Second Position) to support the Atlantikwall. Hitler strongly opposed a heavily fortified Zweite-Stellung in the operational depths of France for fear that it would "magnetically attract" Army units and tempt the Wehrmacht to prematurely retreat. General der Artillerie Walter Warlimont of the Oberkommando der Wehrmacht (OKW) later recalled that any talk of a strategic fortification line deep in France was "taboo" within Hitler's inner circle. Hitler's directive to Generalfeldmarschall Rundstedt's Oberbefelshaber West (OB West) on November 2, 1943 permitted the Army to conduct a reconnaissance of a Zweite-Stellung behind the Atlantikwall and to begin modest work using civilian labor, but specifically limited it to tactical fieldworks near the coast and not at operational depths. Only 31 of 88 planned strongpoints were completed prior to the Normandy landings. Regardless of Hitler's opposition, OB West conducted a precautionary reconnaissance of a much deeper Zweite-Stellung in the spring of 1944 and forwarded it to sympathetic officials in Berlin, especially the Wehrmachtführungsstab (WFSt) of the OKW.

The Allied invasion of Normandy on D-Day (June 6, 1944) breached the Atlantikwall in a day's fighting, much to the consternation of Hitler who believed that the fortifications could repulse an amphibious attack, or at least hold it at bay for a few weeks. Future defensive fortification efforts had been substantially undermined by the commitment of so many resources to the failed Atlantikwall. Aside from the enormous amount of concrete and steel that had been used, the Atlantikwall had absorbed most of the Wehrmacht's substantial inventory of captured artillery from the Soviet and French Armies. While most of the Atlantikwall remained in German hands through August 1944, no effort was made to recover any of this equipment. Hitler had begun to adopt a rigid "stand-fast" mentality that would not countenance any withdrawals, including the withdrawal of valuable equipment from idle sections of the Atlantikwall.

By late June, the OKW staff was becoming increasingly concerned about the potential for an Allied breakout from the Normandy bridgehead, and the complete absence of any defensive lines in France. A surreptitious effort was started by the WFSt to plan a defensive line extending from the Somme through to the Marne and finally to Jura in the Alps. During June and July there were bitter debates in Berlin over Germany's strategic options, with many senior Army commanders recommending that Heeresgruppe G (Army Group G) in central and southern France be withdrawn towards the Rhine to create a more defensible shield in Lorraine and Alsace. Hitler was infuriated by such suggestions and viewed them as more evidence of the Army's defeatism. This debate soured Hitler to any major Rhine defense program in the summer.

The failed bomb plot against Hitler on July 20, 1944 led to a further hardening of his attitudes towards strategic withdrawal, his inclination being to link any talk of deep defensive lines with defeatism and the bomb plotters. In late July 1944 the Allied breakout from the Normandy bridgehead plunged the Wehrmacht in France into a deepening crisis. On July 28, Hitler finally consented to creating a defensive line along the Somme–Marne–Saone rivers under the direction of the new military governor of France, General der Flieger Karl Kitzinger, which became known as the Kitzinger-Stellung. In spite of his Luftwaffe rank, Kitzinger had started his military career as an Army engineer, and he would be closely associated with German fortification efforts on the western front through 1945.

The Normandy crisis was further deepened by Operation *Dragoon*, the second Allied amphibious landing on the Mediterranean coast, on August 15. Not only was German control of northern France threatened, but the rapid advance of US and French units up the Rhône Valley threatened to cut off German forces in central and southern France. On August 17 Hitler was obliged to order the withdrawal of Heeresgruppe G, and so plans were changed to extend the Kitzinger-Stellung to link Heeresgruppe B with Heeresgruppe G in Lorraine. Time quickly ran out for the Wehrmacht in France before any significant work on the Kitzinger-Stellung could begin. The last two weeks of August and first two weeks of September 1944 were later dubbed "the void" in

Although very little of the Kitzinger-Stellung was ever completed, a number of reinforced bunkers were constructed in 1943–44 in France well inland of the Atlantikwall. These were mainly hardened headquarters bunkers like this example at Soissons. (NARA)

German accounts as the Wehrmacht was decimated in its headlong retreat back towards the Rhine. The Westwall along the German border became a rallying point for the retreating German troops. By the third week of September 1944 it was becoming clear that the Wehrmacht had already reached its nadir and was beginning to recover its ferocious defensive potential. This abrupt change was later dubbed the "*Wunder am Westwall*" ("Miracle on the Westwall").

Starting the West-Stellung

The July 20, 1944 bomb plot against Hitler had originated with the leaders of the Ersatzheer (Replacement Army), so to squash any future mutinies Reichsführer-SS Heinrich Himmler was placed in charge of homeland defense, becoming Chef der Heeresrüstung und Befehlshaber des Heimatheeres (Chief of Army Mobilization and Commander of the Home Army). In early August 1944 Himmler called together a meeting at Kaiserslautern with the leaders of the western border *Wehrkreise* (military districts) and their staffs along with the *Gauleitere* (Nazi party district leaders) to announce that Hitler had entrusted him with the organization of the defense of the western German border. Himmler's Kaiserslautern meeting started the process of creating a new series of defensive lines along Germany's western borders. On August 5, 1944 the fortification staffs of the western *Wehrkreise* met in Wiesbaden under Generalleutnant Rudolf Schmetzer to plan the construction program. Schmetzer had been the fortification inspector of OB West until early 1944, and had been heavily involved in the Atlantikwall effort. The plan called for a defense zone which was to include the Netherlands, with special emphasis on the immediate erection of a defensive line from Antwerp via Maastricht to Aachen, called the Brabant-Stellung. This line was planned to exploit the Albert Canal by reinforcing it with fieldworks.

The formal start of the West-Stellung can be traced to Hitler's August 24, 1944 Directive Nr. 61. This divided the task of creating the West-Stellung between the *Gauleitere* and the *Wehrkreise*:

> The positions should be constructed in such a way that an uninterrupted system of tank obstacles is created first of all, preparations are made for a demolition zone ahead of the positions, and a continuous and deeply echeloned system of fortifications is built up, which should constantly be reinforced at the most important points. The Metz-Diedenhofen [fortified zone] and sectors of the Maginot Line will be incorporated into our position, the existing installations rebuilt, and those which will not be used should be destroyed.

When Germany reabsorbed Alsace and Lorraine into the Reich after 1940, the Wehrmacht inherited stretches of the Maginot Line. This is Bloc 5 of Ouvrage Simsershof, part of the Ensemble de Bitche that was captured by the Seventh US Army's 71st Infantry Regiment, 44th Division, on December 19, 1944 after several days of intense bombardment. The Maginot Line in this area saw repeated combat, including the US attacks in December 1944, the German *Nordwind* offensive in January 1945, and the US efforts to push through the line into the Saar in March 1945. (NARA)

Hitler amplified his intentions for the West-Stellung with another directive on September 1, 1944, which ordered an extension of the Westwall to the Ijsselmeer in the Netherlands. Construction of the West-Stellung was to be carried out using a levy of the local population as well as the Reichsarbeitdienst (RAD: Reich Labor Service) and the paramilitary construction agency Organisation Todt (OT). Hitler ignored his earlier disapproval of rear defensive lines, but he retained a visceral antipathy to any talk about defenses on the eastern side of the Rhine owing to its association with Army defeatism. A conversation between Hitler and Army chief-of-staff Heinz Guderian at a September 1, 1944 conference at his Wolfsschanze (Wolf's Lair) headquarters gives a flavor of his views at this time:

Hitler: They [Wehrkreis V in the Vosges Mountains] will have to get antitank guns and close-combat weapons because otherwise they will be overrun by tanks in this stretch here. Guderian, there is no worse defense than the Rhine, this has to be repeated again and again!

Guderian: The Rhine is no defense at all. It's nothing compared to the Vosges.

Hitler: The Rhine fortifications are totally outdated, of course.

Guderian: Hardly existing anymore – everything collapsed.

The Wehrmacht's growing interest in fortified lines in the autumn of 1944 stemmed from both tactical necessity and the declining quality of the available infantry troops. The advantages of fortifications when in a defensive posture are self-evident, but the German art of war had always included a subtle recognition of their offensive virtues, as this pre-war Festung-Pionier report noted: "Every fortification has a double purpose, to defend the homeland against enemy attack, but also to offer our military forces a secure and favorable launch point from which to stage an attack."

This viewpoint had special resonance for senior commanders in September–October 1944, after Hitler ordered planning to begin for an early winter offensive in the Ardennes. The West-Stellung had obvious value in the defensive battles of the autumn, but it also served to provide the Wehrmacht with a shield behind which forces could be preserved for the offensive. Fortified lines could be garrisoned with second- and third-rate infantry units while the better Panzer and infantry units were kept in reserve for the offensive. Festungsdienstelle Düren (Düren Fortification Sector) was the scene of the most intensive fortification efforts in September–December 1944 to shield the concentration of forces in the neighboring Eifel region behind the Ardennes.

The Wehrmacht's growing dependence on fortified lines was a tacit recognition of the severe deterioration of German infantry units after the summer 1944 debacles in both the east and the west. The Wehrmacht was able to recover from the "the void" in September 1944 by transferring tens of thousands of Luftwaffe and Kriegsmarine personnel into the Army after their aircraft and ships were idled by the growing fuel shortages. This sudden infusion of troops helped to stem the tide of defeat and was the wellspring of the "*Wunder am Westwall*" in September 1944 when the Allied advance through Belgium was finally halted. Although the young Luftwaffe ground crews and Kriegsmarine sailors were often well motivated, they were thrown into combat with little or no specialized infantry training. Under these conditions, a hurriedly assembled infantry battalion was much more effective

A typical example of a Westwall personnel bunker located near Sevenig-bei-Neuerburg in the Eifel border region. This particular type was designed to accommodate two *Gruppen* – 20 infantrymen. (NARA)

when fighting from carefully prepared defensive fieldworks and bunkers than in open-field combat. Furthermore, the 1944 defeats had chewed up much of the Army's vital tactical leadership, especially the NCOs and junior officers so vital in close-quarters combat. It was much easier for inexperienced NCOs and junior officers to control green troops in trenches. Conditions in the infantry continued to deteriorate through the autumn and into the winter of 1944–45 as the pool of Luftwaffe and Kriegsmarine troops was exhausted, leaving little recourse but to absorb regional militias such as the Landesschützen and Volkssturm into the defense effort.

In 1944–45 the Allies enjoyed a substantial firepower advantage over the Wehrmacht both in terms of field artillery and air power. Field fortifications provided a measure of relief for the German infantry. The West-Stellung substantially enhanced the firepower of the field army (*Feldheer*) by the addition of the numerous machine-gun positions and antitank guns beyond divisional holdings, as well as the long-range firepower of the fortification artillery. The role of the Westwall in halting the Allied advance in the autumn of 1944 encouraged the Wehrmacht to attempt to repeat this success in other sectors by extending fortification lines along the Rhine.

Organizing the defense of the Rhine
One reason that the 1944–45 fortification programs are not well known is that they were created by the Heimatheer (Homeland Army), not the better-known field army tactical formations. The German Army had a separate Ersatzheer, responsible for raising and training units for the field armies. Engineer offices of the Ersatzheer also managed the previous Westwall program, and were responsible for much of the 1944–45 program as well. Germany was divided into 19 *Wehrkreise*; three of these districts (V, VI, and VII) covered the western border on the Rhine and so figured prominently in the West-Stellung program.

Construction of the Westwall had been managed by three principal commands: the Düren Fortification Sector (Festungsdienststelle Düren) under Wehrkreis VI, the Eifel-Saar-Palatinate Fortification Command (Kommandantur der Besfestgungen Eifel-Saarpfalz) under Wehrkreis XII, and the Upper Rhine Fortification Command (Kommandantur der Befestigungen Oberrhein) under Wehrkreis V. By the summer of 1944 there were six fortification commands

(Kommandantur der Befestigungen) in the west: the Dutch Coast (Küste), Lower Rhine (Niederrhein), Eifel, Saar-Palatinate (Saarpfalz), Upper Rhine (Oberrhein), and Vosges (Vogesen). During the autumn of 1944 the sector commands were reduced to five by merging the Dutch Coast and Lower Rhine offices, and most were redesignated as Senior Fortification Commands (Höhere Kommando der Befestigungen). These sector offices coordinated the efforts of the district military engineers, the OT paramilitary construction agency, local Nazi Party offices, and private contractors.

The subordinate defense sectors of the Westwall were managed by a Fortification Engineer Command (Festungs-Pionier-Kommandeur), which was equivalent to a brigade headquarters. These were composed of a Fortification Engineer Staff (Festungs-Pionier-Stab) equivalent to a regimental engineer staff, usually with two Sector Groups (Abschnittsgruppen), which were equivalent to battalion staffs. The number of commands and staffs in each district fluctuated depending on the workload and, in some cases, commands or staffs from interior *Wehrkreise* were transferred to the Rhine districts to assist with the West-Stellung effort. The main function of these organizations was planning, surveying, and overseeing the construction of the fortifications. The actual construction work was done by other organizations.

Since 1942, the Nazi Party *Gauleitere* as Reich Defense Commissars (RVK: Reichsverteidigungskomissare) were responsible for civil defense. In August 1944 Himmler announced plans to expand their responsibilities more broadly to homeland defense. The RVK were responsible for the "Operational Zone" (Operationsgebiet) 12.4 miles (20km) behind the front, while the Army controlled the "Combat Zone." Under the July 19, 1944 Führer Directive, construction of fortifications inside Germany was assigned to the RVK, although supervision remained in the hands of the Wehrkreis fortification staffs. Party involvement in the West-Stellung would prove to be a source of endless frustration for the Army. The *Gauleitere* had no engineering experience and tended to view the construction programs as simply another way to curry favor with party leaders in Berlin.

The task of coordinating the fortification programs of the Ersatzheer with the tactical needs of the field army was undertaken by the OB West's Commander for Fortification Affairs West (Kommandant Festungsbereich West). Hitler's September 9, 1944 directive transferred command of the West-Stellung, including the Westwall, from the local Wehrkreis commanders to OB West, and temporarily subordinated the border *Festung-Pionier* commands to the field command, effective from September 11, 1944. As a result, the OB West fortification department was elevated to the High Command for Fortification Affairs West (Oberkommando Festungsbereich West) and Gen. Karl Kitzinger was appointed its commander, effective from October 5, 1944. It was based in Bad Kreuznach.

The OT had been the primary state bureau for the creation of the Westwall, autobahns, and the Atlantikwall, but the OT was not especially prominent in the construction work on the West-Stellung in the autumn of 1944. The rout of the Wehrmacht in France in the summer of 1944 had led to a massive loss of

Although many of the bunkers along the Westwall had fallen into disrepair, the extensive lines of antitank walls and dragon's teeth remained intact and effective in 1944. (NARA)

OT engineers and workers in France and Belgium, and it was in the process of rebuilding in the autumn of 1944. Hitler directed the OT to other high-priority projects, especially those connected with the reconstruction of German industry in the face of relentless Allied bombing attacks. The OT was also responsible for a massive program to create underground factories for key German military industries. Although not prominent in the West-Stellung effort, the OT did sometimes provide engineers and workers where specialized skills were needed, such as in the construction of major concrete bunkers.

West-Stellung design

The West-Stellung program had barely begun when the US Army began approaching the outer edge of the old Westwall in mid-September 1944 on the approaches to Aachen. This was part of the Düren Fortification Sector, one of only two Westwall sectors with a double set of defensive lines. By the end of November 1944 about half of the original Westwall bunkers were still operational after many had been lost in the Aachen fighting. A German inspection report from November 30, 1944 listed the available positions (see table below).

The September 1944 plan for the West-Stellung envisioned a substantial expansion of the old Westwall to provide defense-in-depth through a series of secondary lines and blocking positions. The plan included the construction of 3,636 combat pillboxes and casemates, 7,999 underground bunkers, 847 observation posts, and 270 command posts with funding of 310 million Reichsmarks. By the third week of September 1944 the workforce had mushroomed to over 400,000, including about 300,000 German civilians and 65,000 foreign laborers, plus various soldiers, OT workers, and other groups. The initial allotment of concrete was about 50,000m^3 per month, and this was gradually expanded to over 500,000m^3 to cover the construction through early 1945. To put this in some perspective, this was about 15 percent as much concrete as had been used in the four-year Westwall program of 1936–40.

The amount of concrete allotment was constrained by the lack of a skilled OT workforce, the onset of the wet and cold autumn weather, and the different focus of the West-Stellung program compared to the Westwall. Instead of depending on permanent concrete bunkers, the West-Stellung consisted mainly of fieldworks supported by antitank ditches and other forms of obstacles. Bunkers and gun positions were usually made of earth and timber and not concrete. This was done for doctrinal reasons as much as it was due to construction problems. A reliance on fighting bunkers was an uncomfortable match with German tactical doctrine. The Westwall had largely been Hitler's idea for strategic political reasons, and was not based on Wehrmacht tactical concepts. German commanders believed that the average infantryman would rather enjoy the relative comfort and security of a bunker than engage in the vigorous activities essential to German tactics. If posted inside concrete bunkers,

Operational Westwall bunkers, November 30, 1944	
Type	**Quantity**
Underground personnel bunkers	4,909
Machine-gun concrete pillboxes with armored embrasures	1,406
Observation bunkers	555
B-Werke with machine gun and armored cupolas	419
Antitank gun garages	252
Artillery and infantry personnel bunkers	231
Artillery bunkers	102
Artillery and infantry ammunition bunkers	82
Medic bunkers	75
Command bunkers	33
Antitank bunkers	6
Total	*8,070*

One of the first steps in rejuvenating the Westwall was the clearing away of several years of foliage and overgrowth that obscured fields of fire. When the US Army first encountered the Westwall near Aachen in September 1944 many of the bunkers were almost completely overgrown, as seen here. (NARA)

infantrymen would cower in them during an attack, leaving them vulnerable to infiltration, isolation, and envelopment. Instead, the commanders insisted that close combat would to take place from open trenches where the infantry had better situational awareness and could use their mobility to counterattack after repulsing an attack. German doctrine was comfortable with the idea of using bunkers as shelter from artillery, but not as the combat focus. This viewpoint was made very clear in a directive from OB West on December 8, 1944 to all commands along the West-Stellung: "Fighting along the Westwall will be conducted from field positions which will be established between the fortifications and bunkers. Bunkers will only be utilized as shelters for the troops during rest periods and as protection from heavy fire when enemy attacks were not imminent. Troops must leave the bunkers immediately in the case of enemy attacks. The only exceptions are fortress infantry and other specialized fortification troops operating weapons which cannot be moved outside."

Another major aspect of the Westwall enhancement was the improvement of antitank positions, since tanks and other AFVs had become a far more central

Many Westwall bunkers had been cannibalized for parts during the construction of the Atlantikwall. This 423P01 armored cupola on a bunker near Hollerath in the Eifel region near the Belgian Ardennes is missing the armored plates for its machine-gun ports. Here it is inspected by a soldier of the US Army's 324th Engineer Battalion, 99th Division, on February 8, 1945. (NARA)

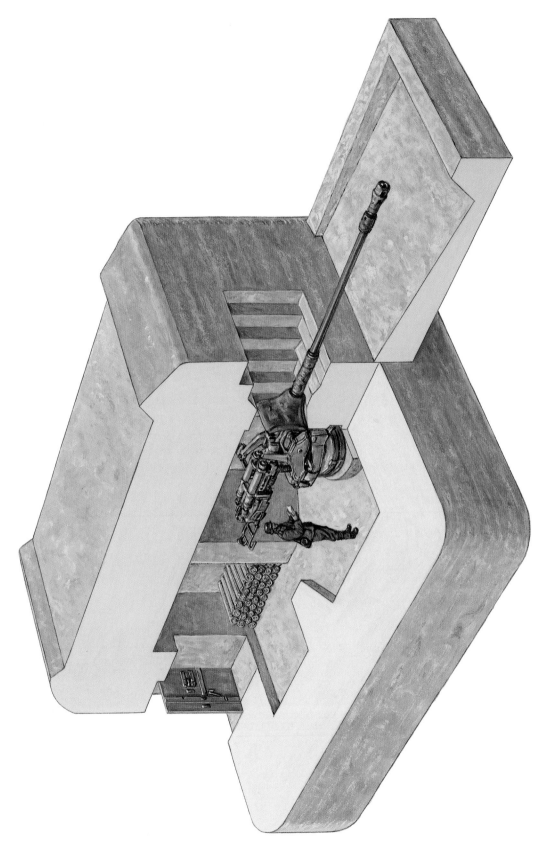

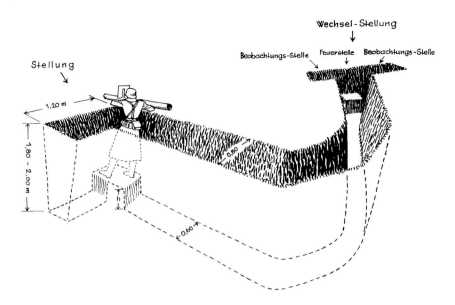

Stellung

1,20 m

1,80 - 2,00 m

Wechsel - Stellung

Beobachtungs-Stelle   Feuerstelle   Beobachtungs-Stelle

An illustration from a Heeresgruppe G pamphlet showing the recommended layout of a Panzerschreck antitank position, consisting of a foxhole on the left for the rocket-launcher crew, and a reserve-position (*Wechsel-Stellung*) trench to the right, which also accommodated the team's observation posts (*Beobachtungs-Stelle*). (NARA)

focus in land combat tactics in the decade after the Westwall's original conception in the mid-1930s. Hitler issued a "Sofort Aktion Panzerabwehr" directive (Immediate Action Tank Defense) to give additional priority to this issue, which is covered in more detailed below (see pp. 25–29). Besides conventional antitank guns, the advent of antitank rockets such as the Panzerfaust and Panzerschreck was integral to the new fortification plans. There was a tactical synergy between these infantry weapons and antitank obstacles. Antitank obstacles such as dragon's teeth, mines, road barriers, and antitank ditches could slow the tanks and force them into predictable channels where they could be destroyed at close-range using the new antitank rockets.

Principles of defense

Wehrmacht fortification lines were generally classified by their role. The primary defensive position along the main line of resistance (Haupt-Kampf-Linie, or HKL) was generally called a "Stellung," which can be translated as a "position" or "line." This term was widely used for everything from a minor trench line to an elaborate fortification program extending for dozens of miles. The more significant positions built under the West-Stellung program were generally identified by geographic names (e.g. Kyll-Stellung, which was positioned along the river Kyll); sometimes they received other names, such as the

---

B   REGELBAU NR. 703 SCHARTENSTAND FÜR 88MM PAK 43/3 AUF SKL IIA, FESTUNGS-PAK-VERBAND XI, PANTHER-STELLUNG, NETHERLANDS, 1945

Ideally, the West-Stellung pedestal antitank guns were supposed to be emplaced in fully protected gun casemates, but in reality the lack of time and resources meant that few of these were constructed in 1944–45. The densest concentration was located in the Panther-Stellung near Utrecht, where at least eight were built. These casemates were based on the Atlantikwall designs rather then Westwall types and have the same characteristics, such as an open front embrasure. The related Rgl. Nr. 677 was designed for the towed PaK 43/41 antitank gun to accommodate the gun trails. The design of the Rgl. Nr. 703 is simple, consisting of a fighting chamber for the gun and crew and two ammunition closets behind. A concrete apron was often poured in front of the embrasure to prevent loose earth or dust from being kicked up by the gun blast. The rear access was protected by an armored steel door, and generally a large earthen berm would be positioned a few yards behind the access door as a glacis to shield it from enemy gunfire. The embrasure would usually be covered by a camouflage net, which would be removed prior to combat, and the roof was covered with dirt and plated with grass to offer some minimal camouflage.

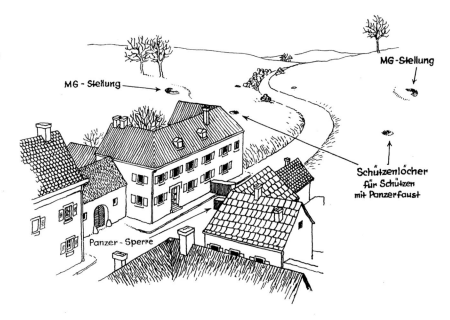

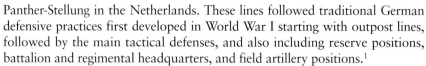

The fortification of towns centered around the use of log *Panzersperren* barriers to slow down enemy tanks so that they could be engaged by antitank rockets. This illustration from a 1944 Heeresgruppe G pamphlet issued to Army and Volkssturm units for the defense of towns and villages shows the usual *Panzersperren* barriers blocking the main street with adjacent foxholes for *Panzerfaust* antitank teams (*Schützenlöcher für Schützen mit Panzerfaust*), shielded by machine-gun positions (*MG-Stellunge*). (NARA)

Pre-fabricated concrete *Brandwachenstände* (fire watch posts) were widely used by the Army for local security tasks, like this example captured after the fighting in Eschwiller in December 1944. They were also the inspiration for the Koch bunker, which had an open top and could be buried as a quick machine-gun pit. (NARA)

Panther-Stellung in the Netherlands. These lines followed traditional German defensive practices first developed in World War I starting with outpost lines, followed by the main tactical defenses, and also including reserve positions, battalion and regimental headquarters, and field artillery positions.[1]

Another focus of the West-Stellung program in the autumn of 1944 was to amplify the old Westwall with *Riegelstellungen*. This term is variously translated as "blocking positions" or "switch positions;" "switch" is an allusion to railroad switch lines. The *Riegelstellungen* were perpendicular to the HKL so that if the Allies broke through the HKL at a weak point, they could not roll up the flanks of the main defensive line. The accompanying West-Stellung map on p. 5 shows the major *Riegelstellungen* but does not identify them individually due to their sheer number.

Besides the major defensive lines, there was a concerted effort to reinforce towns and villages in the operations zone behind the front line, and this was a major focus of the *Gauleitere*. Since there was seldom the time or resources to create elaborate antitank ditches or fieldworks, the most common technique was to frustrate Allied mechanized columns by blocking the main streets through the towns with log *Panzersperren* (tank barriers). There was little expectation that these barriers could actually stop a concerted tank attack for very long, but they could slow down approaching tanks and make them more vulnerable to infantry with antitank rocket launchers. Instructions issued to Army and Volkssturm units regarding the fortification of towns and villages repeatedly stressed the synergy between the obstructions and the antitank rocket teams.

Another standard defensive position on the Rhine was the *Brückenkopf*, or bridgehead. These were defensive belts created on the western bank of the main Rhine cities in order to prevent their capture. These bridgeheads were also used as the focal

---

[1] Standard German tactical defenses are covered in more detail in Fortress 23: *German Field Fortifications 1939–45* (Osprey: Oxford, 2004).

point by German engineer battalions for the establishment of ferry sites; these could be used in the event that bridges were demolished, or used as a secondary means of river crossing in areas where the local bridges could not support heavy equipment such as tanks. The main engineering efforts in 1944 were directed towards the most threatened sectors, especially in Westfalen to shield the Ruhr industrial region and in the Baden region opposite Alsace; the cities in the Rhineland opposite the Saarpfalz received less attention since there was much greater operational depth in front of the Rhine in this area.

This *Panzersperre* in Gevenich in February 1945 is a good example of one of the recommended configurations, which allowed pedestrians and small vehicles access to the road. (NARA)

A major role of these bridgehead defenses was to buy time to ensure that the Rhine bridges could be demolished before their capture by the Allies. Bridge security was a tactical paradox for the Wehrmacht in the autumn of 1944. On the one hand, the Army wanted to avoid the premature demolition of bridges since they were a vital artery for moving troops back and forth over the Rhine. As a corollary, the Allies regarded the demolition of the Rhine bridges as a tactical advantage since the bombing of bridges complicated German reinforcement of the western side of the Rhine, and also trapped German forces where they could be encircled and forced to surrender. In addition, bridges dropped into the Rhine served as major impediments to Rhine river traffic, which was vital for the harried German defense industry in western Germany, especially the Ruhr. As a result, through much of the autumn of 1944 and early winter of 1944–45 the German tactic was to defend the bridges, while the Allied tactic was to destroy bridges when possible. The tactical paradox came to the fore when the Allies began to surge towards the Rhine bridges. At this stage, the tactics reversed; the Wehrmacht wanted the bridges demolished to prevent an Allied crossing of the Rhine, while the Allies hoped to secure a bridge.

For most of 1944 and early 1945 bridge defense centered mainly on antiaircraft defense. This was the responsibility of tactical Army flak units rather than the Luftwaffe's Reich air-defense organizations. Major bridges

One of the most common configurations of *Panzersperre* was this timber type, with the shoulders constructed of a timber box filled with stone or earth and a removable set of horizontal logs forming the center of the barrier. Here, an M10 3in. GMC (Gun Motor Carriage) of the 645th Tank Destroyer Battalion crunches through a *Panzersperre* in Lembach on December 14 during the attack by the 45th Division in the Low Vosges. (NARA)

Battalion defense sector, Scharnhorst-Stellung, Reichswald, February 1945

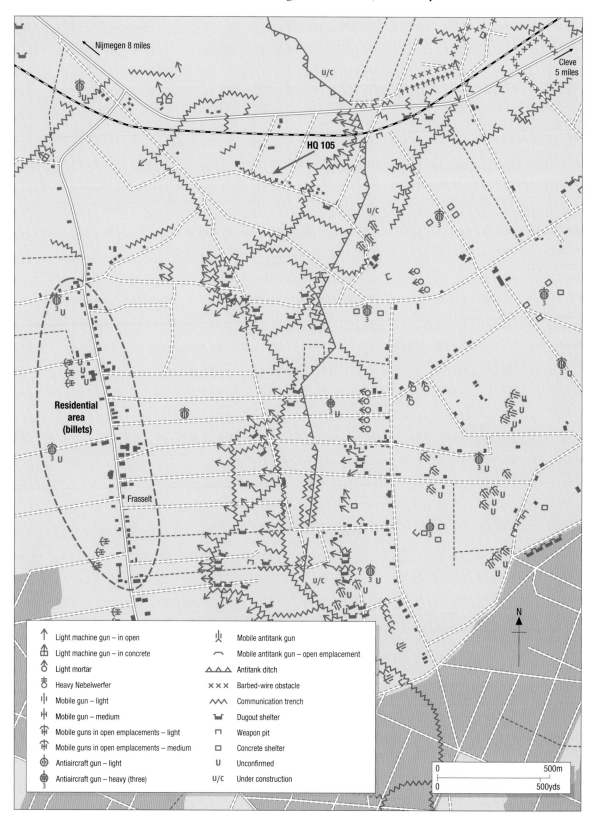

Nijmegen 8 miles

Cleve 5 miles

HQ 105

U/C

U/C

U/C

U/C

Residential
area
(billets)

Frasselt

N

	Light machine gun – in open		Mobile antitank gun
	Light machine gun – in concrete		Mobile antitank gun – open emplacement
	Light mortar	△△△	Antitank ditch
	Heavy Nebelwerfer	×××	Barbed-wire obstacle
	Mobile gun – light	∧∧∧	Communication trench
	Mobile gun – medium		Dugout shelter
	Mobile guns in open emplacements – light	⊓	Weapon pit
	Mobile guns in open emplacements – medium	□	Concrete shelter
	Antiaircraft gun – light	U	Unconfirmed
	Antiaircraft gun – heavy (three)	U/C	Under construction

0	500m
0	500yds

22

such as Cologne or Strasbourg had 88mm flak units, supplemented by 50mm, 37mm, and 20mm batteries. Smaller bridges generally had only the smaller-caliber automatic cannon. In the spring of 1945 some bridge defenses were supplemented with new rocket flak batteries. The other issue of bridge defense was protection against floating mines. Engineer units attached paravanes to bridge pilings, and in some cases anti-mine net barriers were erected. Although the British and American Armies did not make much use of mines to attack bridges, there was use of air-delivered mines to interfere with river traffic, which could also damage bridges. The French 1ère Armée did use mines in attempts to collapse key Rhine bridges during the January 1945 fighting in Alsace to overwhelm the Colmar Pocket.

The preparations needed for the demolition of major Rhine bridges took weeks of engineer work since it was vital to drop large spans into the river or the Allies could simply bridge small gaps with readily available tactical bridging. Engineer units of the Ersatzheer began an extensive program to place explosive charges on the Rhine bridges in September–October 1944, based on instructions from Berlin. However, on October 14, 1944 the Cologne–Mühlheim Bridge (Mülheimer Brücke) was totally demolished during an American air attack when the demolition charges were accidentally detonated. This proved to be a major catastrophe for German industry since the bridge wreckage effectively blocked Rhine river traffic and prevented the shipment of coal and industrial goods. A massive effort was needed to clear the river. New instructions were sent out from Berlin that the actual explosive charges were to be removed from the Rhine bridges but the circuitry left in place. While this avoided the risk of premature demolition, it posed a threat that the charges might not be in place when the Allies reached key bridges. This would be at the heart of the Ludendorff Bridge capture at Remagen, as detailed later (see p. 42).

Besides their role in security for the Rhine bridges, the *Wehrkreise* had traditionally been responsible for control of the waterways to prevent approaching enemy troops from seizing barges and other craft for use in crossing the river. Under a pre-arranged plan, the OKH headquarters would issue the command "Freimachen des Rheine" (Clear the Rhine) along with a particular code, at which point the district commands would clear the Rhine of all river craft and move them into the eastern river tributaries to keep them out of enemy hands.

OPPOSITE PAGE
This shows a typical West-Stellung position in 1945, in this case, a battalion defense position of Grenadier-Regiment 1051 of the 84. Infanterie-Division on February 8, 1945, when they were hit by the 46th Brigade, 15th (Scottish) Division, during the British XXX Corps offensive – Operation *Veritable*. These defenses were overrun in several hours with the infantry supported by flamethrower tanks from the 79th Armoured Division. This defensive line was situated near the northernmost extremities of the old Westwall with the Maas-Stellung to the west and the Geldern-Stellung to the east near Kleve. This particular set of defenses was fairly typical of the 1944 West-Stellung construction and was carried out by Festungs-Pionier-Kommandeur XXI.

The decision of when to drop major Rhine bridges to prevent their capture was often a source of tension. German combat units wanted them kept open as long as possible to allow units to retreat, while Berlin insisted that none fall into Allied hands. The massive Hohenzollern railway bridge at Cologne was finally detonated around noon on March 6, 1945 after the commander of LXXXI Armee Korps, Generalleutant Ernst Baade, personally intervened. Two days later, procrastination in triggering the demolition charges at the Ludendorff Bridge at Remagen led to the capture of the only major bridge over the Rhine. (NARA)

The Air Defense Zone West (LVZ West) flak positions were created in parallel to the Westwall in the late 1930s. Although under Luftwaffe control, these flak batteries frequently played a prominent role in defense efforts in the 1945 fighting, like this emplaced 88mm battery in Neuss, part of the Brückenkopf Düsseldorf defenses. Protected niches for the ammunition have been created using concrete sewer pipe. (NARA)

Allied paratroop capabilities caused considerable concern in Berlin. The principal approach to this threat was for the *Wehrkreise* to create alert units from local resources, which could be rushed to the scene of a landing as an initial step to contain it until the field army could mobilize the regular forces. The July 15, 1944 Führer Directive instructed the Ersatzheer to raise combat groups and alarm units in the border *Wehrkreise* that could be activated under the codeword "Gneisnau." In the wake of the failed Operation *Market Garden* airborne assault in September 1944, the October 19, 1944 Führer Directive reiterated the need to prepare to deal with the Allied airborne threat along the Rhine and granted permission for the Ersatzheer to control non-military security forces such as railroad and postal guards under the earlier "Gneisnau" plan. There were some efforts in the autumn of 1944 to build up anti-glider obstacles in likely landing areas, but the potential sites were so many and the resources so slim that only a modest number of areas

Several Rhine bridges were protected from air attack by the secret new Flakwerfer 44 Föhngeräte, which fired a salvo of 35 73mm unguided rockets, depending on volume of fire rather than accuracy for its effect. This example served with 3./Flak Ausbildungs-und-Erprobungs Batallion 900 in Erpel near the Ludendorff Bridge at Remagen, where it was captured along with the bridge. Behind it is a US Army M16 antiaircraft halftrack of the 634th AAA Battalion (Automatic Weapon) guarding the bridge area. (NARA)

received such attention, mostly in the Lower Rhine area and the Netherlands.

Arming the West-Stellung

The Westwall had been thoroughly stripped of weapons for the Atlantikwall program, and so there was a desperate need for weapons. At the beginning of October 1944 the three border *Wehrkreise* had about 1,940 machine guns, but the existing bunkers required 5,120. In September 1944 all Luftwaffe, Kriegsmarine, and OT units east of the Rhine were ordered to turn in 100 percent of their machine guns and 90 percent of rifles; those between the Rhine and the Westwall were to give up 50 percent. The principal types of machine guns allotted to the West-Stellung were the World War I MG-08 and the newer MG-34. Some Luftwaffe MG-151s were adapted to the fortification role and a program was begun to permit the use of the common MG-42 machine gun in embrasures originally designed for the MG-34, which had a smaller barrel.

The Allied use of airborne glider tactics in Normandy and at Arnhem in 1944 prompted some efforts to erect anti-glider obstacles, like these examples at the Leeuwarden airfield in the Netherlands being inspected by a Canadian soldier of the 9th Infantry Brigade on April 16, 1945. (LAC PA-131560)

The Westwall rejuvenation's most pressing need was for antitank guns. The existing Westwall PaK (Panzerabwher Kanone: Antitank gun) bunkers had been configured around the 37mm PaK 36 or in later cases, Czech 47mm guns. These were obsolete but in any case often had been removed. In September 1944, Oberst Hermann Öhmichen from the Generalinspekteur der Panzertruppe office was assigned to determine if the existing Westwall antitank bunkers could be rearmed with 75mm guns. A survey of about 700 Westwall antitank bunkers found that about 200 weren't worth the effort since their guns were intended for short-range flanking fire. Of the remainder, about 335 were potential candidates for conversion to 75mm PaK 40 guns. Ideally, the bunkers needed a new armored embrasure for the gun; these were difficult to manufacture, transport, and install so in the event only about 100 bunkers were rearmed with the 75mm PaK 40. Since the old Westwall bunkers could not easily accommodate the larger guns a series of new gun bunkers were developed, patterned on the types used in the Atlantikwall such as the Regelbau 703 Schartenstand (construction standard 703 embrasure bunker) for the 88mm gun.

Festung artillery regiments in most sectors in 1945 were no longer deployed in concrete bunkers, but were in static emplacements. This 20.3cm Haubitze 503/5(r), the German designation for the captured Soviet B-4 203mm Howitzer M.1931, was deployed near Sarrebourg with Festung-Artillerie-Abteilung 1528 for defense of the Lower Vosges. It was emplaced under an elaborate camouflage cover resembling a small farm building, which has mostly been stripped away in this view after the battery was overrun by the Seventh US Army in late November 1944. (NARA)

A novel source of antitank weapons for the West-Stellung emerged after Allied strategic bombing of German Panzer factories made several hundred guns redundant. Hitler became enamored of the concept of quickly turning these into improvised antitank guns to create a defensive belt behind the main line of resistance to stop any Allied tank penetrations. These weapons were assigned to special *Festungs-PaK-Verbande* (fortification antitank units), and a September 16 Führer Directive specifically forbade the deployment of these units in the front lines. These new formations were raised in the border *Wehrkreise* and varied in size, some only consisting of a staff to administer existing gun batteries, while others were relatively large with several new gun companies, each with a dozen antitank guns.

In the rush to arm these new formations, a variety of simple pedestal mounts, or *Sockellafetten* (SK-L), were hastily designed and manufactured by

Festungs-PaK-Verband units

Location	Military District	Festungs-PaK-Verband	Formation	Composition
Lower Rhine	Wehrkreis XI	Festungs-PaK-Verband XI	December 1944	Staff only
Aachen	Wehrkreis VI	Festungs-PaK-Verband XIV	December 1944	Staff only
Saarpfalz	Wehrkreis XII	Festungs-PaK-Verband XII	December 1944	8 gun companies
Black Forest	Wehrkreis V	Festungs-PaK-Verband XXVI	January 1945	14 gun companies

One of the fundamental problems of the pedestal-mounted antitank guns was their vulnerability due to lack of concrete or armored protection. As a result camouflage was usually the only recourse, as seen on this SK-L IIa 88mm KwK 43/3 mounted on a concrete pad. This gun was derived from that used in the Jagdpanther, and is still fitted with its distinctive armored mantlet. (APG)

Rheinmetall-Borsig's plants in Düsseldorf and Unterlüss. Ideally, these could be bolted to pads inside the new PaK bunkers, but the difficulty of creating enough new bunkers meant that they were usually deployed in open revetments. This had obvious shortcomings, so later batches of guns were mounted instead on a simple cruciform steel mounting, the *Behelfskreuzlafette* (improvised cruciform mount), which could be repositioned if necessary. Some *Festung* troops nicknamed these new weapons "Panther guns" (*Pantherkanonen*), even though none came from Panther tanks. By late 1944

C BETONFUNDAMENT FÜR SKL IIA MIT 88MM PAK 43/3 JAGDPANTHER, FESTUNGS-PAK-VERBAND XIV, RUHR-STELLUNG, FEBRUARY 1945

This is a typical example of a fieldworks gun pit for a *Pantherkanone*. It consists of a simple earthwork pit, wide enough to permit easy gun traverse and with enough room for the crew and ammunition, with a concrete pad constructed in the center. These guns were usually deployed in open fields to cover large swathes of surrounding terrain, so some form of camouflage was needed. One common method was to create a camouflage tent from triangular timber frames covered in camouflage nets, which would then be pushed away by the crew prior to combat action, as seen here. The guns were delivered to the *Festung* units by subcomponent, so the weapon is painted in a variety of colors including the usual ivory AFV interior color on the main gun assembly, red-lead primer on some parts such as the gun mantlet and counterweight, standard dark-yellow camouflage paint on other parts such as the main gun housing and muzzle break, and heat-resistant grey paint on the gun tube.

This is an SK-L Ia pedestal-mounted 50mm KwK 39/1 Bordkanone, derived from Luftwaffe heavy fighters such as the Me-410. As can be seen, the pedestal mount was quite crude. (NARA)

about 2,000 pedestal guns had been ordered, including 400 50mm KwK 39/1 Bordkanone aircraft guns, 700 short 75mm L/24 guns (KwK 51 and KwK 67), 250 long-barreled 75mm Pak 40s, 450 Kwk 43/3 Jagdpanther 88mm guns, and 50 88mm Kwk 43 King-Tiger guns with plans to complete them by mid-March 1945. In addition, more than 500 regular 75mm Pak 40 guns on the normal wheeled carriage were earmarked for mounting in bunkers and special fieldworks. Not all of these weapons were directed to the West-Stellung, as a similar fortification effort was underway in eastern Germany to deal with the threat of the Red Army; most of the short-barreled 75mm guns were earmarked for the east while the 88mm guns were earmarked for the west.

The first large-scale deployment of the fortification antitank guns took place in October 1944 in the construction of the Vosges and Belfort Gap defenses, when an initial allotment of 58 *Pantherkanonen* was made. The Panther-Stellung in the Netherlands also received some of the early shipments of these weapons. By the end of November 1944 over 80 of the Jagdpanther guns had been deployed on concrete pads, but over 30 were lost when the Vosges defenses were overrun. The loss of Strasbourg on November 25, 1944 put the Allies firmly on the Rhine and greatly alarmed Hitler. This prompted

A modest number of Regelbau 20 PaK-bunkers were modernized in 1944–45 but substituted the 75mm PaK 40 for the earlier 37mm or 47mm gun, like this example in the Wiseembourg Gap in 1945. (MHI)

West-Stellung PaK front 1945					
Mount	Gun	Source	Allotment	Combat ready, Jan 18, 1945	Combat ready, Feb 15, 1945
SK-L Ia	50mm KwK 39/1	Me-410s, heavy fighters	150	25	82
SK-L Ic	75mm K51, KwK 67	SdKfz 234/3s, other	300	132	11
SK-L Id	75mm Pak 40/3	fortification versions	80	0	25
Rad-lafette	75mm Pak 40	towed AT guns	370	141	177
SK-L IIa	88mm KwK 43/3	Jagdpanthers	450	153	252
SK-L IIa	88mm KwK 43	Kingtigers	50	0	0
Total			**1,400**	**451**	**547**

a Führer Directive on November 28, 1944 calling for a crash program for antitank defense (Sofort-Aktion Panzerabwehr). Hitler insisted that the Upper Rhine and Saar fronts receive special attention, with at least 100 Jagdpanther guns going to the Saar defensive line from Merzig to the Rhine and 90 more along the Upper Rhine.

The antitank guns were not evenly spread along the West-Stellung, but concentrated in the most vital sectors. For example, during the construction of the Panther-Stellung in the Netherlands in September 1944, five batteries of 88mm guns were provided. During the reinforcement of the Ruhr-Stellung in January and February 1945 about 160 88mm guns were emplaced. About 300 antitank guns were emplaced during the Upper Rhine defense effort in late 1944 to early 1945, mainly in the Germersheim–Karlsruhe area. Besides the dedicated pedestal guns, the defensive lines were amplified by the use of surplus antiaircraft guns, especially the ubiquitous 88mm flak and captured Soviet 85mm guns.

Although most of the pedestal guns were mounted on concrete pads, some were fitted to a *Behelfslafette* improvised cruciform mount like this SK-L IIa 88mm KwK 43 of Gruppe Müller of 5./Festungs-PaK-Verband XVIII, knocked out by the US 14th Armored Division near Bergzabern in the Wissembourg Gap north of Steinfeld during the late March 1945 fighting. The trunnion for this gun is completely missing. (Patton Museum)

One of the principal problems in reinforcing the Rhine defenses was the shortage of heavy artillery. The disastrous summer 1944 campaign had led to the loss of nearly all of the 4,900 field guns deployed in France and the Low Countries, as well as the 3,800 large-caliber guns positioned on the Atlantikwall. Besides these many field guns, the Atlantikwall had also consumed vast amounts of antitank guns in the 37mm–50mm range. An October 1944 survey in the border *Wehrkreise* located 932 field guns of 41 different types; this inventory was reinforced by guns from districts further inside Germany. These weapons armed the *Festung-Artillerie-Abteilungen* (fortress artillery units) that were gradually assigned to the West-Stellung. By early 1945 there were 35 of these deployed along the West-Stellung, substantially reinforcing local firepower. Indeed, in the most heavily contested sectors of the West-Stellung the *Festung-Artillerie* often doubled or tripled the artillery firepower available to infantry divisions. In spite of their designation, very few of these batteries were deployed in concrete fortifications as there were only 256 artillery

A significant number of flak guns were assigned to the Rhine PaK front. Some, like this one, were surplus Luftwaffe weapons that were issued to *Festung-PaK-Abteilungen* with a *Behelfslafette* cruciform mount. Unlike the normal cruciform mount, this inexpensive frame was designed for fixed use only, and the gun was no longer mobile after it was deployed. This example saw combat in the fighting for the Cologne bridgehead in early March 1945. (NARA)

This Pantherturm I on an OT-Stahlunterstand Type D was being emplaced by Festung-Pionier-Kommandateur XIX, 3 miles (5km) west of Bonn along Highway 56, but was captured by the US Army before it was finished in 1945. This example uses the *Ostwallturm*, which was based on the Panther tank turret but with thicker roof armor and other changes. A second steel box containing the crew quarters would be positioned underneath the fighting compartment box seen here, and the entire assembly buried, leaving only the turret exposed. (NARA)

casemates in the Westwall; by 1945 the designation essentially meant that the formation had no organic transportation and so was immobile.

Rhine Panzer-Stellung

The problems of fortifying the pedestal guns and the vulnerability of the guns mounted in open revetments prompted consideration of other alternatives. Surplus French tank turrets had been widely used on the Atlantikwall, and a design based on the Panther tank turret had been developed in 1943. The *Pantherturme* proved to be a better antitank fortification than bunkers since the gun and crew were far better protected than when in bunkers with open

Obsolete PzKpfw I turrets were recycled for fortification use by adding a thicker front armor plate as the Festung-Panzer-Drehturm 4803. A total of 143 of these were deployed in the West-Stellung, mainly in Festungsdienstelle Düren along the Roer. This particular example was captured by the US Army 30th Division during the fighting near Niederzier, part of the Ruhr-Stellung north of Düren on 26 February 1945. (NARA)

D HOLZSTAND FÜR PANTHERTURM, FESTUNGS-PAK-VERBAND XII, SAARPFALZ, MARCH 1945

Lack of time and resources led to the use of improvised wooden substructures (*Holzunderstande*) for many of the *Pantherturme* that were emplaced in early 1945, also nicknamed as *Schnelleinbau* or "fast construction." These timber structures were deep enough to provide elementary crew quarters including a heater, as well as a niche in the rear for ammunition storage. Access was usually through a door on the right side that was shielded by a trench. This particular example is an *Ostwallturm*, which was one of the custom-built turrets with thicker roof armor and a modified mantlet. These turrets lacked the usual turret drive system, so an alternate drive system could be provided on the floor under the turret or the turret could be fitted with supplementary manual traverse mechanisms.

The *Pantherturm* could also be deployed on a Regelbau 687 concrete bunker. This is the original trial bunker at the Hillersleben Proving Ground and it uses a recycled Panther Ausf. A turret rather than the dedicated *Ostwallturm*. (MHI)

This is a view of the Krab MG-Panzernest in the vertical position, showing the machine-gun embrasure in the front. This is a captured example sent back to the Aberdeen Proving Ground for technical evaluation, probably from those captured in Alsace in November 1944 during the Vosges campaign. (APG)

embrasures, they offered complete traverse compared to the limited traverse from bunkers, and they were small and inconspicuous targets. There were two sources of Panther turrets: they were either cannibalized from damaged or worn-out tanks, or they were custom-produced *Ostwallturme* (East Wall turrets) with thickened roof armor. There were plans to produce a hundred *Ostwallturme* a month by late 1943, but the low priority afforded to fortification work meant that this plan was reduced to only 15 a month by the end of January 1944. The *Pantherturme* was deployed initially in Italy in April 1944 and proved to be highly effective in the defense of the Gothic Line. Although better known for its role in Italy, the *Pantherturm* was much more extensively used in the Rhine-Stellung, though with far poorer results.

The original configuration, called the Pantherturm I, was deployed on a pre-fabricated two-story underground steel structure developed by the OT to speed construction in remote locations. A total of 143 were manufactured in this configuration, of which 119 were allotted to the west. As an alternative, a conventional reinforced-concrete bunker was designed in May 1944, called Regelbau 687. There were significant problems building these complicated structures in remote mountain areas such as the Vosges and on the Rhine plains due to cold and wet weather. A simpler underground timber bunker was developed locally among the Rhine-Festung *Pioniere* in November 1944.

In the Vosges defensive line, 49 *Pantherturme* were allotted by November 1944. However, the Allied offensive struck before any of the turrets were completed, and only two concrete bunkers had been poured. At least one turret and some other components were lost. In the Aachen area, work started in September 1944 with plans to deploy 40 *Pantherturme* with 17 on concrete bunkers and the rest on steel. Three fortification

The Krab MG-Panzernest was designed as a quick way to emplace a machine-gun pillbox with minimal engineering support. The armored cupola was delivered upside down with a wooden towing limber connected to a machine-gun embrasure in the front. After a suitable trench was dug, the crew would simply tip over the contraption into the hole. These examples were intended to be deployed in the Vogesen-Stellung near the Saales Pass but were captured by the Seventh US Army in November 1944 before they could be deployed. (NARA)

companies were deployed in this sector to man the turrets: Festung-Pantherturm-Kompanien 1201, 1202, and 1203. Due to the intense fighting with the US Army along the Ruhr-Stellung, 20 of the steel sub-structures were overrun prior to installation and the program was stalled. As a result, the program shifted its focus and planted the turrets further east along the new Erft-Stellung. A combination of the weather and combat conditions delayed the progress of the program. At least two turrets were hastily emplaced on the Ruhr-Stellung in late January 1945 but one quickly flooded. By mid-February only one was ready for combat and the other 30 sites under construction were overrun during Operation *Grenade* in late February 1945. The seven surviving turrets were ready for action by early March 1945, though some were missing components. One was hastily emplaced in Siegburg in the suburbs south of Cologne.

The Saar region was the third area to receive the *Pantherturm*, starting in late December 1944. These were built in two clusters, a group of 11 for Festung-Pantherturm-Kompanie 1204 in the Hardt mountains north of Saarbrücken and 20 more for Festung-Pantherturm-Kompanie 1205 covering the Wissembourg Gap (Weissenburger Senke, or Zabener Senke) on the west bank of the Rhine. When Operation *Undertone* was launched on March 15 by the Allied 6th Army Group, 23 of the 31 turrets were combat-ready. Details of their combat history are lacking and they were quickly overrun in the late March 1945 fighting.

After the failure to deploy the *Pantherturm* in Alsace, Festungs-Pionier-Kommandeur I shifted its attention to the eastern bank of the Rhine as part of the Black Forest fortification effort. A total of 30 Pantherturm IIs were emplaced on wooden sub-structures in March 1945 in spite of lingering problems with the supply of parts. They were manned by Festung Pantherturm-Kompanien 1207 and 1208 but there is little evidence regarding their combat use in the 1945 fighting against the French 1ère Armée.

Old PzKpfw II light-tank turrets were rearmed with surplus 37mm guns and deployed as the Festung-Panzer-Drehturm 4804. This example is mounted on a Regelbau 283 bunker at the Hillersleben Proving Ground. This is a rear view of the bunker showing the lower access door; in combat the front of the concrete bunker would be completely enclosed in earth. (MHI)

Besides the *Pantherturme*, a large number of obsolete PzKpfw I and PzKpfw II turrets were modified for fortification use. Improved PzKpfw I turrets were designated as Festung-Panzer-Drehturm 4803 and 143 were assigned to the west. Festungs-Pionier-Kommandeur XIX allotted 55 of these to the Eifel and 40 for the Lower Rhine, but only 44 had been completed by February 1945. The larger Pz.Kpfw II turrets were modified, becoming the Festung-Panzer-Drehturm 4804, substituting a 37mm gun. A total of 60 of these were deployed in the west, often mounted on Regelbau 238 bunkers; at least 25 were lost by February 1945. Another armored turret used in the Rhine defensive lines was the MG-Panzernest, a small armored steel pillbox first deployed in Italy and Russia in 1943 as a means to quickly build up a defensive position. It was small enough to be towed into position using a normal transport truck, and after a shallow pit was dug it could be emplaced by a few men with no special equipment. A total of 50 MG-Panzerneste were shipped to the West-Stellung, all for the AOK 19 (Armeeoberkommando 19) sector on the Upper Rhine, but many were lost in November 1945 when the Vosges defenses were overrun.

THE LIVING SITES

Building the West-Stellung

The chaos in the autumn of 1944 along Germany's western border precluded the construction of large numbers of concrete bunkers. Most construction in 1944–45 involved fieldworks such as trenches, antitank ditches, and weapon revetments. They were reinforced here and there by a few concrete pillboxes, some fixed antitank guns on concrete pads, and the occasional *Panzerturm*. Once the senior headquarters had approved the establishment of a defensive line, the regional Festungs-Pionier-Stab would assign one of its survey companies to visit the site and plan the layout both on maps and by marking the terrain using pegs and other common engineering techniques. The extent of construction can be appreciated from this tally:

West-Stellung fieldworks through February 25, 1945	
Length of defensive lines	1,458 miles (through Dec 25, 1944)
Tank traps and obstacles	820 miles
Trenches	5,866 miles
Barbed-wire obstacles	1,732 miles
Bunkers	11,797
Koch (pre-fabricated) bunkers	5,516
Gun and AT-gun firing positions	5,326
Machine-gun and mortar positions	75,092
Infantry and artillery observation posts	1,092
Machine-gun and mortar tobruks	1,244
Heavy-mortar positions	36
Antitank ditches	320,239
Antitank mines	28,676
Antipersonnel mines	22,365

The workforce was mostly conscripted from local districts by the *Gauleitere* as part of the Volksaufgebot (Peoples' Contribution) program. Since virtually all able-bodied men had been drafted into the Wehrmacht by this stage of the

war, the labor levies were almost invariably young boys from the local Hitlerjugend and old men. In some districts women were also recruited, though this was usually frowned upon by Berlin. The Festung-Pionier-Stab in each district contained several labor supervision companies, consisting of an officer and 16 NCOs, who instructed the draftees and supervised the work. General der Artillerie Herbert Loch, who directed the Eifel Fortification Sector, described his experiences:

When the improvement of local strongpoints accelerated in December 1944 into the rear areas up to the Rhine, the local civilian population was obliged to cooperate, chiefly in the construction of antitank obstacles. The *Gauleiter* was responsible for the requisitions associated with the construction work. The effectiveness of the work parties varied widely due to the variable attitudes of the inducted workers. The numbers of workers promised seldom showed up; they were often less than half! In reports to higher headquarters, the *Gauleitere* often listed the numbers of workmen on the project that were purely the product of fantasy. Progress on the site was slowed by the erratic supply of labor. In many cases, if not as a general rule, the work on the site began eight to ten days after the assignment of the mission, even if it was only 15–20km by march. The workers were supposed to be fed by the *Gauleitere*. East of the Rhine, the rationing system had been disrupted by events and so the Heeresgruppe ordered the Army to supplement the food of the civilian

workers. Usually the work was located 10km or more behind the front. If the battle-line drew closer, the civilian draftees were sent to other sites further to the rear and the work taken over by special Army work squads.

General der Infanterie Franz Mattenklott attributed many of the problems to the ambitions and technical incompetence of the local *Gauleitere*:

> Repeatedly, their amateurish games with engineering had to be rectified to bring it in line with the actual needs of border defense. Their ruthless employment of inadequately supplied men, women, and children was the result of their rivalry to show "which district had recruited the most people… The senseless overburdening of the people gave rise to crises, increasing the anger of the laborers. Without hesitation, the Party authorities blamed the Army engineer staff. Fortunately, the people knew who was to blame.

The scale of these projects was quite enormous and they became major civic events. By the end of September 1944 the daily workforce had expanded to 470,000 people, of whom about 350,000 were ordinary civilians. On average, about three-quarters of the workforce were German civilians, about 15 percent were conscripted foreign laborers, and about 3–4 percent were soldiers. The scale of the work effort tapered off in the late autumn due to poor weather and the increasing hazards of working near the front lines. The workforce fell below 200,000 around Christmas 1944, and reached its nadir of 115,000 workers in late January 1945 due to the cold weather. It began to rebound in February 1945 because of the new work on the Rhein-Stellung.

Many of the trench lines dug for the West-Stellung contained log-reinforced shelters so that the infantry sections could take cover during artillery bombardment. The soggy autumn weather of 1944 led to conditions reminiscent of World War I trenches. (NARA)

The most common projects for unskilled labor involved antitank ditches and trench lines. The standard engineering calculation for digging antitank ditches was that it took a team consisting of one officer and ten supervising soldiers along with 100 workers between 37 and 68 days per kilometer (0.62 miles) of antitank ditch. The difference in time depended on the type of ditch and the amount of soil that had to be removed, varying between $7,500m^3$ and $13,500m^3$. The construction of the Ruhr-Stellung east of Aachen took nearly three months and involved on average between 20,000 and 25,000 workers; the neighboring Erft-Stellung required about 40,000 men. The Kyll-Stellung involved about 12,000 for three months, and the Autobahn-Stellung in March 1945 involved more than 20,000 workers. Even a relatively small position, the Alf-Ahr-Stellung, required 8,000 men for over a month. The work on the Vosges mountain defenses in the autumn of 1944 involved about 40,000 workers, and the Upper Rhine fortification projects used another 40,000.

When there was no convenient source of civilian labor, or when the construction was too near the front lines, military manpower was used, generally from rear-area units, but sometimes dedicated engineer construction battalions. For example, during the Vosges mountain construction, the labor came from security battalions, police units, Cossack and Georgian formations, and field disciplinary battalions. The December 1, 1944 Führer Directive instructed that supply troops and rear-area service troops were to construct fortifications whenever possible, and were to be used to man rear-area fortifications instead of being billeted in villages.

Aside from the labor issues, the weather posed unrelenting problems due to the wet autumn of 1944, which saw twice as much rain fall as usual; trench lines and antitank ditches were often flooded and this sometimes rendered them useless. On December 29, 1944 the chief of the OKH staff reported that inundation and subsoil water, especially along the Ruhr and Erft rivers, had decreased the defensive value of fortifications and that due to labor shortages they could not be repaired. The hard winter weather that began with heavy snowfall before Christmas created another set of problems, burying many defensive lines in the Eifel under snow. February 1945 saw a return of late-winter rain and the February 22 Führer Directive instructed that in areas where ground and water conditions were likely to lead to quick deterioration of the fieldworks, only fortifications likely to be occupied in the near future would continue under construction.

Troops for the West-Stellung

The Wehrmacht had specialized Festungs-Infanterie and Festung-MG battalions for the Westwall, but these units shrank considerably after 1940. The nominal table of organization for the Westwall was for a garrison of about 200,000 troops, but by mid-1943 there were only 15,715 troops assigned to the fortifications. By October 1944 they had been reduced in strength to only 14 infantry, 37 machine-gun, and 20 Luftwaffe fortification battalions. Besides the combat fortification units, the Wehrkreise also created fortification cadre troops (Festungs-Stamme-Truppen), which were technical troops used to operate the Westwall's specialized equipment. They were quite few in number, totaling only about 4,600 men in early 1945. The majority of these units, over 3,750 men, were deployed in the Saarpfalz sector to operate both the Westwall fortifications and the sections of the Maginot Line absorbed by the West-Stellung program.

The Wehrkreise were responsible for occupying the defensive lines until the arrival of the field army's troops, so the West-Stellung was usually thinly garrisoned by rear-area troops or militias while still in the operational zone behind the combat area. The West-Stellung was built in a modular fashion, corresponding to normal divisional and regimental sectors. However, the regular infantry units assigned to take over the defense of the West-Stellung often never arrived, and so the combat mission fell to rear-area units. Since these units are not as well known as the conventional infantry divisions, it is worth taking a quick look at the variety of such formations, which sometimes saw combat on the West-Stellung in the final months of the war.

The Wehrkreise had a variety of military units under their jurisdiction. Each district had one or more "depot" divisions, which were training units used to build or rebuild infantry divisions for the field army. These were composed

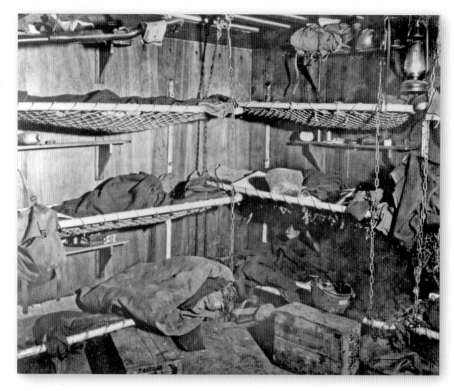

Life in a Westwall bunker was cramped, cold, and damp, but a world better than living in a muddy trench. This is a view inside a personnel bunker near Aachen on September 28, 1944, occupied by US troops. (NARA)

of replacement and training battalions (*Ersatz und Ausbildungs Batallione*) to train new troops, and convalescent companies (*Genesendenkompanien*), which helped wounded soldiers return to combat duty. The *Wehrkreise* also organized alarm battalions from administrative and rear-area support troops, which could be mobilized in the event of an emergency. For local security, the *Wehrkreise* deployed Landesschützen regiments and battalions, which were composed of older soldiers not fit for regular combat units, often World War I veterans in their late 40s. These were supported by local *Landespionier* engineer units, which were responsible for preparing the Rhine bridges for demolition and the operation of ferries to help evacuate troops from the west bank of the Rhine. None of these formations were intended for combat use, but in the desperate days of 1945 they were often sent into action. Besides the military units in the rear areas, there were often police and other paramilitary security units that could be mobilized. The Rhine area was especially rich in specialized units such as river police and customs police (*Zollgrenzschützen*) units.

The most controversial unit involved in the 1945 fighting was the Volkssturm. After the July 20, 1944 bomb plot, Martin Bormann, the head of the Nazi Party, urged Hitler to put his faith in the enthusiasm and fanaticism of a "people's army" (Volkssturm) to master the crisis facing the Third Reich. The Volkssturm was formed under Nazi Party control on September 25, 1944 over the objections of the Army, which felt that a poorly trained militia would have little combat value. The Volkssturm was recruited from any able-bodied men not already conscripted into the military, and so usually consisted of old men and boys. Although the Volkssturm proved effective in many cases on the eastern front, their record in the west was poor. Volkssturm units were primarily intended for the defense of their own towns and villages. The chief-of-staff of Heeresgruppe B, Generalmajor Carl Wagener, offered a jaundiced view:

The Volkssturm was the last, grotesque improvisation of the [Nazi] Party in the desperate effort to fend off a superior, well-equipped enemy. Untrained and poorly led, armed only with short-range antitank and infantry weapons, the Supreme Command unreasonably expected these units to provide last-ditch defense of the homeland. These forces were to be used as close as possible to their own homes. But with their innate common sense, they chose to avoid the dreadful consequences of a futile last stand; when given a choice, they refused to fight. When thrown into action away from their homes, they ran away after the first shot was fired. This was first experienced at Trier, where it resulted in the speedy capture of the city. The subsequent assignment of the Volkssturm companies to regular divisions did little to raise the low military standards of this organization.

A TOUR OF THE SITES

This section surveys the Rhine defenses from north to south. In the north, Heeresgruppe H had been added on November 10, 1944 to take over responsibilities for most of the Netherlands opposite Montgomery's British-Canadian 21st Army Group and thereby freeing-up the neighboring Heeresgruppe B to prepare for the Ardennes offensive. Heeresgruppe B was the largest of the three army groups in the most critical sector, from the Lower Rhine near the Netherlands through the Eifel and along the Rhine through the Saar as far as Trier; it faced Bradley's American 12th Army Group. Heeresgruppe G's sector started at Trier in the Saarpfalz and ran through Alsace and the Black Forest to the Swiss border, facing Devers' Franco-American 6th Army Group.

Lower Rhine defenses: Heeresgruppe H

In the wake of the Operation *Market Garden* attack towards Arnhem there was some concern that the British 21st Army Group was intending to break into Germany by a northern route, and so a new defensive line, the Panther-Stellung, was created by the KBN in October 1944 to block a northward drive along the eastern side of the Ijsselmeer. In the event, the Panther-Stellung protected against a contingency that did not occur. The September 30, 1944 Führer Directive ordered the construction of a second defensive line behind the Dutch Westwall extension between the Ems and the Rhine on the German side of the frontier.

During December 1944 and January 1945, the Ardennes battles to the south provided Heeresgruppe H the time to deepen defenses for an anticipated British winter offensive out of the Nijmegen area southeastward towards Wesel on the Rhine. The Westwall was not strong in this area so attention focused on a sequence of north–south blocking positions, the Kellenriegel through the Reichswald, followed by the Niers-Ruhr-Stellung stretching from Kleve southwards towards München-Gladbach (now called Mönchengladbach). The defensive lines

The Niers-Ruhr-Stellung was constructed between the Maas and Rhine in the autumn of 1944, including a stretch near the Hochwald. This line included about 60 fixed antitank gun sites, like this SK-L Id with the 75mm PaK 40/6. This particular gun on the edge of the Hochwald near Üdem was captured during a skirmish with Canadian infantry of Company C, the Essex Scottish Regiment, on March 1, 1945 in which Major F. A. Tilston won the Victoria Cross. (LAC PA-113683)

On March 5, 1945 Canadian infantrymen of the Queen's Own Cameron Highlanders inspect a Panzerschreck 88mm antitank rocket launcher left behind in a German infantry trench, part of the Niers-Ruhr-Stellung near the Hochwald. This is typical of the type of infantry defensive positions created in the autumn of 1944 as part of the Lower Rhine defense effort. (LAC PA-131254)

played a significant role during Operation *Blockbuster*, the February–March 1945 Rhineland offensive. The final defensive positions in the Rhine foreground were a series of bridgehead defenses near the main Rhine cities. Brückenkopf Wesel was constructed in the bend on the western bank of the Rhine. This was reached by the First Canadian Army on March 10, 1945 and reduced in conjunction with the neighboring Ninth US Army.

The most extensive Heeresgruppe H bridgehead was the Erweiterter Brückenkopf Duisberg-Düsseldorf (Reinforced Bridgehead Duisberg-Düsseldorf), which was intended to shield the Ruhr industrial zone. This consisted of an outer defensive line stretching from the Rhine near Dinslaken down past Krefeld and finally to Düsseldorf. Inside this outer belt, each of the four major river-crossing areas received their own defensive lines: Brückenkopfen Homberg, Duisberg, Ürdingen, and Düsseldorf. The Ruhr bridgehead line stretched across the boundaries of both Heeresgruppen H and B. This was struck by the Ninth US Army's Operation *Grenade*, starting on February 23, 1945, which penetrated the Düsseldorf bridgehead by March 1 and reached the Rhine on March 5. The final blows in this sector were Operations *Varsity* and *Plunder*, a combined airborne and river-crossing operation on March 24, which broke through the Rhine defenses around Wesel.

Lower Rhine and Eifel defenses: Heeresgruppe B

Heeresgruppe B had the most extensive and complicated defensive line in northwestern Germany. This sector was especially important since it blocked access to the Ruhr industrial region and shielded the preparations for the planned Ardennes offensive. It was the site of the most intensive fighting along the former Westwall in the autumn of 1944, dubbed the Siegfried Line Campaign in official US Army histories.[2]

This area included most of the old Festungsdientstelle Düren of the Westwall and stretched from the Düsseldorf bridgehead southward to the Trier Flankenstellung (flanking position) on the Germany–Luxembourg border. Aachen was shielded by two layers of Westwall defenses: the initial Scharnhost-Stellung, which started at the border, and the Schill-Stellung east of the city. This sector was the initial focus of Bradley's 12th Army Group attacks towards the Rhine. The initial border defensive line was breached almost immediately and the city was taken in October 1944. After capturing Aachen, the First US Army had attempted to push up through the Stolberg Corridor past the Hürtgen Forest to seize the Roer (Rur) dams. As soon as the Westwall was penetrated in September extensive efforts began in order to create new fortification lines to prevent the rest of the Westwall from being rolled up on either flank. This started with a complicated series of switch positions in the southern portion of the defensive line near Monshau and the Hürtgen Forest. The new Ruhr-Stellung, sometimes called the Schlieffen-Stellung, was created along the Roer near Düren and continually reinforced in October–November 1944. One of the major impediments to the construction of defenses in this area

---

[2] This campaign is covered in more detail in Campaign 181: *The Siegfried Line 1944–45: Battles on the German Frontier* (Osprey: Oxford, 2007).

An SK-L IIa pedestal 88mm KwK 43/3 gun from the Jagdpanther tank destroyer mounted on a standard *Betonfundament* concrete pad. This gun was part of the Ruhr-Stellung, deployed in a field near Erkelenz, and was knocked out during the fighting on February 26, 1945 during the Ninth US Army's Operation *Grenade* offensive. The wooden framing was part of a frame for camouflage netting erected over the gun before it was prepared for action. (NARA)

was the unusually rainy autumn weather and the shallow water tables near the many rivers. On the other hand, the Wehrmacht was able to deliberately flood some lowlands as a means of blocking and channeling the US attacks.

Immediately behind the Ruhr-Stellung was the C-Stellung, which stretched about 50 miles (80km) from the Cologne suburbs to Wittlich where it bifurcated into the Kyll- and Wittlich-Stellungen. A major PaK front was created behind the Ruhr-Stellung with roughly 160 88mm guns on concrete pads. Behind the C-Stellung was the Erft-Stellung from Düsseldorf to Bad Godesberg, and within this defense sector were three large bridgeheads: Brückenkopfen Düsseldorf, Köln (Cologne), and Bonn. To further strengthen the defense, several major blocking positions were also erected: the Rheindahlen-Riegelstellung north of München-Gladbach and the Euskirchen-Riegelstellung west of Bonn.

The Eifel region opposite the Ardennes in Belgium had an extensive section of the Westwall still intact, and this had been reinforced sequentially by the Prüm-Stellung and Kyll-Stellung along these rivers. These lines came under attack in February 1945 after the failure of the Ardennes offensive and the subsequent push by Hodges' First US Army and Patton's Third US Army into the Eifel region. As a result, a third line, the Wittlich-Stellung emanating off the C-Stellung, was under construction in March 1945, but it was overrun before completion. This was the sector where the first major breach of the Rhine defenses occurred when the First US Army captured the Ludendorff Bridge at Remagen on March 9. The unexpected capture of this bridge provides evidence of the inherent problems in the German 1945 defense scheme. Hitler's directive to "stand-fast on the Westwall" tied the main forces

A view inside a Festung-Panzer-Drehturm 4803 on February 26, 1945, near Niederzier, part of the Ruhr-Stellung north of Düren. It shows another change made to the original PzKpfw I turret: the addition of armored covers over the front two turret flaps, which permitted the flaps to be opened for ventilation while at the same time protecting the occupant from bullet splash. (NARA)

in the sector to an overextended and vulnerable defensive line. When the US 9th Armored Division penetrated the defensive line, it was able to race to the bridge much faster than the German infantry divisions in this sector could react. There was exceptionally poor coordination between the field army and the Ersatzheer rear-area formations in the sector, and the bridge had not been completely prepared for demolition. The bridge was shielded by a completely inadequate garrison of Landesschützen and Volkssturm men, who failed to contest the American advance.[3]

A typical log antitank roadblock, part of the Kyll-Stellung near Kyllberg, Germany being surmounted by troops of the US 318th Infantry Regiment, 80th Division on March 9, 1945. (NARA)

The Saarland: Heeresgruppe G

The southern flank of Heeresgruppe B where it met Heeresgruppe G on the Moselle was the Trier-Flankenstellung, a traditional fortification zone for many centuries because it was the guardian of the Moselle Gate, which commanded access to the heart of Germany. The Saar-Palatinate region southeast of Luxembourg had been a traditional invasion route into Germany via the Moselle Gate, and so had an extensive array of classic fortification zones. Aside from Aachen, this was the only section of the Westwall with a double defensive line that covered Saarbrücken. Following France's defeat in 1940 Germany once again absorbed Lorraine and Alsace into the Reich, along with it the fortification zones that had been modernized by the Kaiser's army in 1870–1918 around Metz and Diedenhofen (Thionville). The Metz fortresses blocked Patton's Third Army for most of October and November 1944.[4] German fortification efforts in this sector in 1944 were focused on amplifying the extensive Westwall fortifications along the old 1918–40 border with additional new defensive lines.

The defense in the Saarpfalz sector was awkwardly reinforced by the Maginot Line fortifications on the former French side of the border. The Maginot Line forts were not ideal for protecting the German frontier since obviously they were oriented in the other direction, but many weapons had full traverse and numerous infantry shelters were useful regardless of the original intent. German engineers conducted an extensive survey of these fortifications in 1941 and conceived a scheme to reorient the defenses to protect the German frontier; these studies remained on paper. The only major change was the addition of underground cabling linking the old French communication system into neighboring German networks. In 1944 Hitler ordered another survey to determine which complexes could be useful and he ordered that any that were ill-suited to incorporation into the German defensive lines should be blown up.

---

[3] This incident is covered in considerably more detail in Campaign 175: *Remagen 1945: Endgame against the Third Reich* (Osprey: Oxford, 2006).

[4] The Thionville-Metz fortification complex is detailed in Fortress 78: *The German Fortress of Metz 1870–1944* (Osprey: Oxford, 2008).

The Wissembourg Gap was one of the major blocking positions in the Saarpfalz region. This is an antitank bunker located in that sector showing the 75mm PaK 40 antitank gun that had been located within. (NARA)

Like the Westwall, the Maginot Line was cannibalized for weapons and components for the Atlantikwall. The Maginot Line forts in this area were partly reoccupied by the Wehrmacht in November 1944. The Maginot Line from Metz to Hagenau saw extensive fighting in December 1944 during the Seventh US Army's drive into the Low Vosges, with the Bitche ensemble around this old fortress city resisting the initial US attacks.

With the start of the Ardennes offensive on December 16, 1944, Heeresgruppe G conducted a diversionary offensive, Operation *Nordwind*, which started on January 1, 1945. Some Maginot bunkers that had fallen into American hands in the Hagenau sector were attacked and recaptured in the January 1945 *Nordwind* offensive. When the offensive was crushed in late January 1945, AOK 1 was deployed along the Maginot Line with the old Westwall behind it. There were extensive Westwall fortifications around Saarbrücken and in the Wissembourg Gap, and these had been substantially improved under the West-Stellung program. Due to the heavy casualties

An excellent example of the final 1939 configuration of dragon's teeth seen here in the Wissembourg Gap in March 1945. The barrier begins with a reinforced concrete wall followed by dragon's teeth of increasing height. The road here was blocked by a swinging steel barrier, which has been opened by Seventh US Army engineers. (NARA)

Blocking the passes through the High Vosges mountains was the primary objective of the Vogesenstellung program in October 1944. This camouflaged emplacement was apparently the first step in emplacing one of the *Pantherturm* tank turrets to cover this sector of the Saales Pass. (NARA)

suffered in the *Nordwind* offensive, AOK 1 was poorly prepared to resist the inevitable American assault. Forces were so thin that the Maginot Line and Westwall defenses were manned at a level well under half of the intended strength, with single divisions holding areas of front line meant for two.

The attack against AOK 1 in the Saar came from two directions: an assault by Patton's Third US Army from the west and by Patch's Seventh US Army from the south. The push into the Saar began against the Orscholz-Riegel on January 13, 1945, hoping to crack open the Westwall defensive line. The US infantry gradually ground through the weakly manned German defenses, and by mid-February were able to take the Trier defenses from behind, helped in no small measure by its anemic Volkssturm defense. This gained access behind Saarbrücken's double Westwall defensive line, which AOK 1 engineers attempted to close with blocking positions fortified with *Pantherturme* and 88mm antitank guns.

In the south, the dense line on the Alsatian plains south of the Wissembourg Gap was still located along the trace of the Maginot Line, with a reinforced Westwall behind. These defenses were every bit as dense as those in Festungsdienstelle Düren, which had held up the US Army for many months in September 1944 to February 1945, but the troops behind the defenses were substantially weaker. Once the US offensive began on March 12, 1945 the AOK 1 positions quickly became untenable. Hitler had imposed a "stand-fast or die on the Westwall" directive, and German units that obeyed were quickly infiltrated and trapped as the US forces raced to the Rhine. An example of this fighting is provided in more detail below in the "The Sites in Battle" (see pp. 48–61), which examines the fate of the defensive line in the Wissembourg Gap. The Wehrmacht defenses in the Saarpfalz were overrun in a week's time, dubbed the "Rhine Rat Race" by US troops. Once past the fortification lines, the bridgehead defenses on the west bank of the Rhine were completely inadequate due to the lack of sufficient troops, numbering a handful of infantry battalions on a front more than 25 miles (40km) wide. During the last week of March 1945 the Rhine was breached from Frankfurt to Mannheim by VIII Corps in the Rhine Gorge south of Koblenz, north of Oppenheim by XII Corps, at Worms by XV Corps, and at Mainz by XX Corps.

Alsace: Heeresgruppe G

The fourth Rhine defense sector, the Upper Rhine under the control of Wehrkreis V, was shielded on the west bank of the Rhine by the Vosges mountains in Alsace. Prior to 1940 Alsace had been heavily fortified by France as part of the Maginot Line, but these fortifications played little role in the 1944–45 defense schemes. A plan to reinforce this sector had been discussed at a meeting in Wiesbaden on April 5, 1944 with the various fortification staffs, and a defensive line was planned by the Vosges survey staff (Erkundungsstab Vogesen) of the Kommandantur der Befestigungen Oberrhein. Berlin showed little enthusiasm for the scheme and resources were limited because of the heavy commitment of the OT to the Atlantikwall.

This Panther turret was intended for emplacement in the Saales Pass in November 1944 on a concrete bunker, but was overrun before completion. This is an example of a *Pantherturm-Stellung* based on a surplus tank turret rather than a newly produced *Ostwallturm*. (NARA)

The situation changed dramatically in August 1944 with the Operation *Dragoon* landings in southern France and the subsequent retreat of Heeresgruppe G up the Rhône Valley towards the Upper Rhine Valley. The April 1944 plans were dusted off and the small survey staff was enlarged into the Höhere Kommando der Befestigungen Vosgesen (Vosges Senior Fortification Command). Fortification work began in the Vosges using a labor draft starting on September 1, 1944. Hitler held out high hopes for the Vosges as an impregnable defensive line and the fortification plan was formally supported by a Führer Directive on September 27, 1944.

A shortage of concrete and steel reinforcing bar led to the extensive use of underground log construction in the Vogesenstellung, like this underground personnel bunker covering the Saales Pass. (NARA)

The Vosges defenses were intended to consist of three distinct elements. An initial defensive line, variously called the Vor-Vogesenstellung (Vosges Foothills Line) or Vogesen-Randstellung (Vosges Perimeter Line) was located on the western slopes of the High Vosges mountains. These were primarily focused on sealing key mountain passes providing access to the Rhine Valley. It was reinforced by the Vogesenstellung (main Vosges line), also called the Vogesen-Kammstellung (Vosges Ridge Line), deeper in the Vosges mountains. No army in modern times had succeeded in attacking over the Vosges, so this defensive line was expected to be highly effective. The major concern was the Belfort Gap in the south. This was the traditional route into the Rhine Valley and allowed an attacker to advance into the Upper Rhine basin, avoiding the formidable barrier of the Vosges mountains. The Belfort Gap defenses consisted of three sequential blocking positions: the Belfort-, Mühlhausen-, and Kolmar-Riegelstellungen, and two substantial bridgeheads: Brückenkopfen Neuenberg and Breisach. The city of Strasbourg was declared a *Festung*, and received an extensive defensive belt. This sector was held by AOK 19.

Much of the fortification work in the Vogesenstellung was incomplete when the Seventh US Army overran the area in November 1944. This is an antitank gun bunker with the framing for the gun embrasure and most of the steel reinforcing bar in place prior to pouring the concrete. It was part of the defenses intended to block the Saverne Gap. (NARA)

The Allied 6th Army Group attacked the Vosges defenses in late October, before they had been completed. The Seventh US Army overcame both Vosges mountain defensive lines and debouched onto the Alsatian plains in mid-November 1944, while the French 1ère Armée penetrated the Belfort Gap and reached the Rhine on November 19, 1944.

The comprehensive and unexpected failure of the Vosges defenses created a crisis in Berlin since it posed the first opportunity for the Allies to cross the Rhine. As a result, Hitler issued his November 28 Directive, freeing up precious antitank guns and other scarce resources to bolster the Rhine defenses. The commander of the 6th Army Group, Lietenant-General Jacob Devers, intended to bounce the Rhine near Rastaat in late November, but was ordered instead to continue northward on the west bank into the Low Vosges to relieve pressure on the flank of Patton's Third Army.

While these schemes unfolded on the western side of the Rhine, engineers of Wehrkreis V began the first extensive fortification effort on the eastern bank of the Rhine. The Westwall in this area was located immediately along the eastern bank of the Rhine and was modernized as the Oberrheinstellung (Upper Rhine Line) with additional antitank-gun defenses. In contrast to the Heeresgruppen H and B defenses further north, Hitler permitted an extensive fortification effort in the Black Forest on the eastern side of the Rhine due to the unexpected Allied threat on the Rhine in that area. This sector was the only one in Germany with an existing deep defensive line, the Neckar-Enz-Stellung east of Karlsruhe and the Wetterau-Main-Tauber-Stellung (WMTS) following those rivers to the east of Frankfurt. These two programs had begun in 1934 and predated the better-known Westwall as a means to block a French attack. The late 1944 defensive program was called the Hochrhein-Stellung (High Rhine Line) and consisted of a sequence of defensive lines in the mountains east of the Rhine, starting with the Schwarzwald-Randstellung (Black Forest Perimeter Line), followed by the Schwarzwald-Kammstellung (Black Forest Ridge Line). Deeper still were the Donau-Neckar-Stellung (Danube-Neckar Line) from the Swiss border to Pforzheim, and, deeper still, the Schwäbische-

An SK-L IIa pedestal 88mm KwK 43 gun on a standard Betonfundament concrete pad positioned in the Saverne Gap in the High Vosges to block access to Phalsbourg as part of the Vogesenstellung. This position fell during the fighting with the Seventh US Army in November 1944, one of 32 of these guns lost in this campaign. (NARA)

Albstellung (Swabian-Alb Line). Besides the work along the Rhine, the October 8, 1944 Führer Directive ordered the construction of defenses along the Swiss border starting north of the Swiss city of Basel and continuing down along the northern shores of Bodensee to Friedrichshafen. Work on this Alemanen-Stellung was conditional on the completion of the Vosgesen-Stellung, and on February 5, 1945 construction was discontinued to free up its 11,000 workers to aid in the Upper Rhine fortification effort.

The main problem with the Upper Rhine defense scheme was not the fortification effort, but the battered state of the Army in this sector; AOK 19 was decimated in the Colmar Pocket in late January 1945 and its remnants retreated over the Rhine in February 1945 in a very depleted state. Patch's Seventh US Army, instead of jumping the Rhine at Rastatt as planned in November 1944, finally crossed the Rhine near Worms on March 26 alongside Patton's troops. The French 1ère Armée took on the task of clearing the Black Forest. Lacking sufficient engineer assault equipment, 2e Corps d'Armée avoided the heavily fortified bridgehead defenses around Karlsruhe and crossed the Rhine instead between Mannheim and Karlsruhe, starting on March 30. The defensive belt shielding Karlsruhe was avoided and the city was attacked from the north; its Volkssturm garrison was routed on April 4. The Neckar-Enz-Stellung was outflanked from the north by the Seventh US Army above Heidelberg, and then penetrated by both American and French units during the first week of April. The French operations isolated the bulk of AOK 19 in the Black Forest, and it was enveloped and gradually overcome later in April with the new Hochrhein-Stellung lines mostly outflanked from the north.

The Rhein-Stellung

With the failure of the Ardennes offensive in January 1945 the threat greatly increased that the Allies would break through the West-Stellung and cross the Rhine. In spite of his earlier antipathy to constructing defenses on the eastern bank of the Rhine, on February 15, 1945 Hitler ordered the construction of a new Rhein-Stellung from Emmerich to Karlsruhe. This was intended to shield the Ruhr industrial region and was to be amplified by an obstacle zone 18.6 miles (30km) in depth extending in the line Münster–Hamm–Hagen–Remscheid, with the strongest sector between Emmerich and Königswinter. Correspondingly, construction on the west bank of the Rhine was to be stopped. In reality, the sodden late-winter weather and the start of Allied offensives along the Ruhr in late February 1945 prevented much work on the Rhein-Stellung from ever being completed. The only area with comprehensive defenses was the Black Forest, as mentioned above. Most of the other defensive lines on the eastern bank of the Rhine were rapidly overrun by Allied forces in March 1945 before they were completed.

THE SITES IN BATTLE

The fighting along the West-Stellung lasted from the first US Army attacks on the Westwall near Aachen in September 1944 on through the great Rhine-crossing battles of March–April 1945. Many of these battles have already been described in detail in Osprey's "Campaign" series. With such limited space, this section focuses in detail on one engagement: the fight for the fortified village of Steinfeld in the Wissembourg Gap in late March 1945. This battle was selected as it is fairly typical of the experiences along the West-Stellung in 1945 and because it was so amply documented both in text and photographs.

The Wissembourg Gap is located on the Franco-German border immediately west of the Rhine city of Karlsruhe. The sector was heavily fortified by both France and Germany in the late 1930s, with the Maginot Line in French Alsace and the Westwall across the Moder in Germany. The Wissembourg Gap is a natural channel to the Rhine plain, flanked on the east by the Hagenau Forest and Beinwald (Bein Woods) along the Rhine, and on the west side by the forested hills leading to the Haardt mountains.

The Westwall was constructed in this area in the 1938–39 period and received an unusually dense array of fortifications to block the corridor. This sector was designated as Korpsabschnitt S IV (Corps Sector S IV), a two-division

The Westwall bunkers in Steinfeld were camouflaged to look like ordinary rural buildings. This German propaganda photo was taken on January 3, 1940 and shows an artillery bunker armed with a World War I vintage FK 16 77mm gun in Steinfeld, camouflaged to resemble a barn. (NARA)

front including Divisionen Sk and Sl. These unit designations do not refer to actual divisions or corps but were simply place-holders until actual corps and divisions were assigned to the defenses. The corps sector was roughly 25 miles (40km) wide, stretching from Dahn in the east to Budenthal in the west. There were about 1,500 bunkers in this section of the Westwall, about double the average density, with a planned garrison of 18,000 troops. The 4.3-mile-wide (7km) Wissembourg Gap was a regimental sector with an intended force density of 8,000 men, 500 machine guns, and 120 antitank guns. This meant an average of one infantry battalion for each 600–700m of front, one machine gun

A view down the main street in Steinfeld shows the log road barrier removed. A careful examination of the building at the end of the street reveals a machine gun in Stand 234 covering passage along the street. (NARA)

every 14m, and one antitank gun for every 60m of front. Prior to the 1945 fighting the defenses were overseen by an *Überwachungsgruppe* (overwatch group), which was sufficient only to patrol the area and was not strong enough to defend against a major attack.

The Westwall in this sector was under the jurisdiction of Wehrkreis V, so its Festung-Pionier-Stab 9 based near Landau began an effort to rejuvenate the existing fortification line in the late autumn of 1944. In December 1944 the local corps attempted to create tactical defensive lines forward of the Westwall using available divisional resources, but accomplished very little in January due to the intense fighting. The relative lull in February permitted considerable engineering work south of the Westwall, prior to the American March offensive. On February 10, 1945 the OKW instructed OB West to re-examine the construction of obstacle zones along the West-Stellung, with particular attention to the vital Wissembourg Gap.

The fortified area had become overgrown since Westwall construction was completed in 1939, so fields of fire had to be cleared of vegetation.

E   NEXT PAGE: INFANTRY-SECTION TRENCH, 1945

This illustration is based on a Heeresgruppe G booklet issued to troops in 1944–45. This is a typical trench (*Gräben*) for a *Gruppe* (section/squad), in which a 1944 Volksgrenadier rifle platoon would have one NCO and eight enlisted men. This is smaller and less elaborate than typical 1918 trenches, although the basic layout and features would be familiar to troops from World War I. The zigzag shape is to limit the avenues of fire should enemy troops enter the trenches. The section frontage was typically 100–130ft (30–40m) and would be part of a larger platoon and company position. In contrast to hastily dug fieldworks prepared by the troops themselves, this type of trench was typically the product of specialized rear-area engineers and civilian work gangs as described elsewhere in the book. These formal fieldworks usually had the walls of the trench reinforced with wood fascines to prevent them eroding from rain; the bottoms would have a rough flooring, drainage, and grenade pits. Two three-man wooden bunkers (Holzunterschlupfe für

3 Männer) (see inset **1**) are built into the front of the line for temporary shelter; deeper in, the positions would usually be more substantial with larger timber bunkers (B-Stellen aus Rundholz) for resting in. This section contains two command positions (*Führung-Stellunge*) (see inset **2**): the forward one for the assistant squad leader, to serve as the main section observation post, and one slightly deeper in the position for the squad leader, to permit him to oversee the position. These positions typically could accommodate up to three men. On the right side of the position is a dedicated stand for light or heavy machine guns (Feuerstellung für le. oder s. MG). This typically included a platform for mounting the MG 42 tripod in cases where a heavy machine gun was in use (see inset **3**). Wire was stretched over the top of the trench for the attachment of camouflage, and often logs or timbers would be placed over some sections for further cover against artillery airbursts and strafing by enemy aircraft.

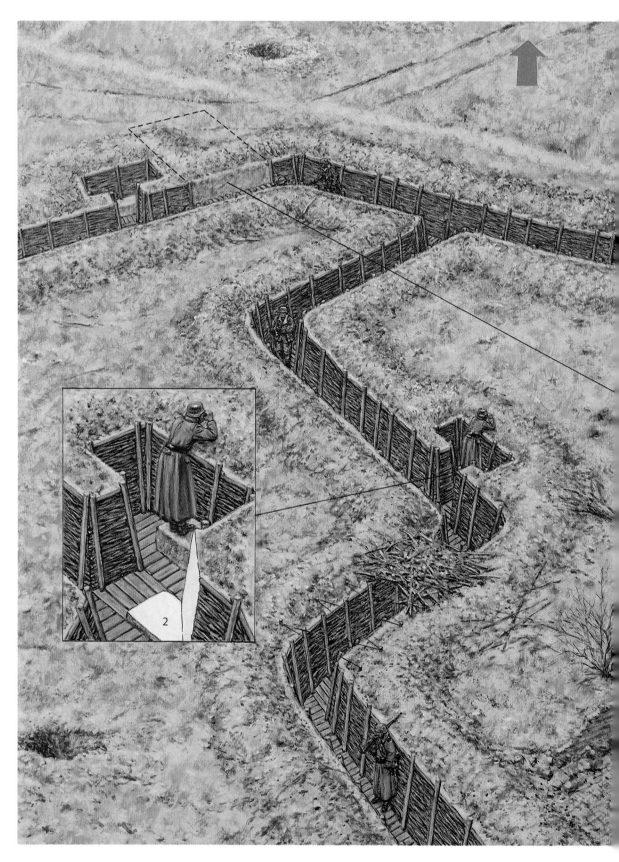

2

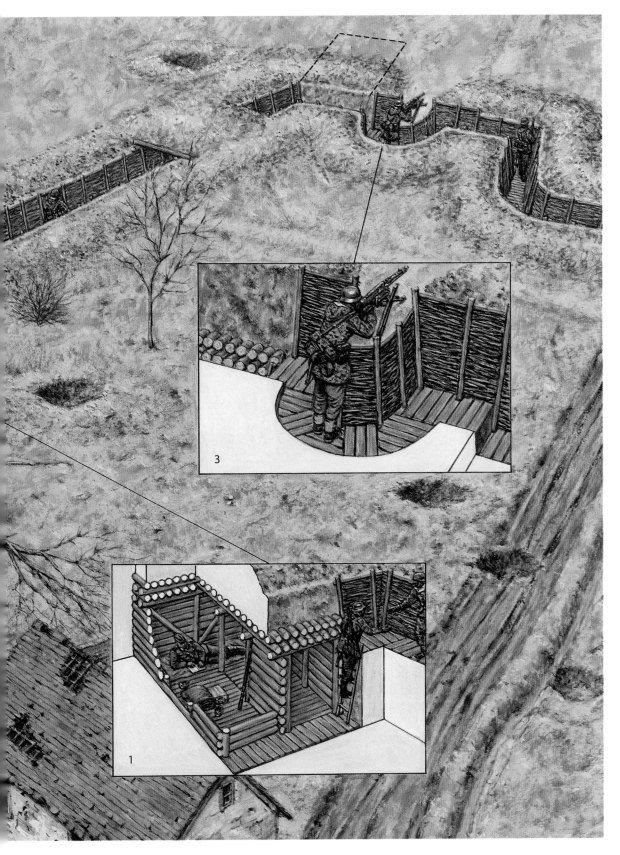

1

3

Stand 234 in Steinfeld was a camouflaged machine-gun bunker, which could fire down the main street of the town. The embrasure was covered by a pair of swinging wooden doors, seen open here on either side of the embrasure. (NARA)

Nearly all of the barbed wire had been stripped away for the Atlantikwall, but recreating barbed wire obstacles was greatly limited by a shortage of material. The pre-war minefields had been stripped away in 1940–41. In Korpsabschnitt S IV there had been roughly 38,000 antitank mines and 21,000 other mines in 1940, for a total of about 60,000. The engineers managed to plant new minefields, including 4,000 antitank mines and 23,000 antipersonnel mines, for a total of 27,000 in 1945. The Wissembourg Gap received 500 antitank mines and 400 antipersonnel mines for a density of only about 210 per mile (130 per kilometer). The engineers also created additional antitank ditches.

The Wissembourg Gap was covered by the 245. Infanterie-Division to the west and the 905. Volksgrenadier-Division to the east, with the latter covering the Steinfeld sector. The 905. Volksgrenadier-Division had been hastily formed the previous spring and had originally been called Division z.b.V. Rässler ("z.b.V." standing for "*zur besonderen Verwendung*," which translates as "for special purpose"). It was rebuilt in January 1945 from the improvised 553. Volksgrenadier-Division, which had taken heavy losses in the Operation *Nordwind* fighting in January 1945. The divisional main line of resistance was held by its two regiments, Kampfgruppe Marbach to the west and Kampfgruppe Giesecke in the Steinfeld area. Oberstleutnant Giesecke had previously commanded Polizei-Abteilung 2, a territorial air-defense police unit. The *Kampfgruppen* consisted of three battalions each. The first battalion deployed in this sector was Volkssturmbattalion Kurpfalz 40/3, commanded by SA Standartenführer König, a World War I artillery *Hauptmann*. Unlike most Volkssturm units, it had already seen some limited combat in the Metz fighting in the autumn of 1944 and again in Alsace in December 1944 to January 1945, mainly in a rear-area role. Due to its limited combat effectiveness, its four companies of roughly 110 men each were spread among the other battalions with one being stationed in Steinfeld. The sector west of Steinfeld was held by Einheit Sarnow (Sarnow's unit), led by Schutzpolizei Major Sarnow with about 200 men from II./SS-Polizei Batallion. A few days before the battle, the Steinfeld sector was assigned to Einheit Wagner, more formally known as Oberrheinisches Grenadier Batallion IV, an improvised militia unit. A French report on the unit described Hauptmann Wagner as "a man of about 40, quite obese, with heart problems." The battalion had a strength of about 300 men armed with old rifles and only three light machine guns per company, with "only about 20 percent ready for the campaign… but nevertheless their morale was not as low as would be supposed." The men in the unit were 40–47 years old from the Baden-Baden area and came originally from driver-training units. They were hastily organized into three companies, with two march companies (A.33 and A.34) stationed in the town and a third company to the rear as a reserve. In total, Steinfeld was defended by about 400–450 troops, made up of 210 soldiers in Wagner's two march companies, 110 Volkssturm

Another example of a well-camouflaged machine-gun bunker is Stand 230/10 in Steinfeld. The machine-gun embrasure is evident in the niche below the overhang, with an armored door on the other side. (NARA)

men, and an assortment of *Festung* troops and a regimental heavy-weapons company in the pillboxes.

The bunkers in this sector had not been as thoroughly cannibalized for guns as in sectors closer to the North Sea, so many of the gun bunkers still had their weapons. These bunkers had been built relatively late and so were mostly armed with the Czech 47mm antitank gun and old FH 16 field guns. The *Festung* troops assigned to the Steinfeld regimental sector were from Kompanie Albers of I./Festungs-Stamm-Abteilung 9 (fortification cadre regiment). This company assigned five to six men to the major pillboxes, and 15–20 men to each B-Werke. This sector was also allotted two batteries of pedestal–mounted 75mm and 88mm guns manned by Gruppe Müller of 5./Festungs-PaK-Verband XVIII. These supplemented a company of four 75mm PaK 40 antitank guns in the immediate Steinfeld defense. The PaK front behind Steinfeld also contained five *Pantherturme* mounted on wooden bunkers: two near Dierbach, two near Vollmersweiler, and one immediately behind Steinfeld. These turrets were manned by Festung-Pantherturm-Kompanie 1205. The regiment in this sector was also supported by Panzerkompanie Gekerle with four tank destroyers, probably JagdPanzer 38(t) Hetzers. Heavy artillery support came from two batteries from Festung-Artillerie-Abteilung 1507, one north of Freckenfield and the other near the regimental command post in Dierbach. They were armed with captured Soviet 122mm and 152mm howitzers.

The Seventh US Army first reached the German border in this area in December 1944, and small US spearheads reached as deep as Steinwald before being repulsed. The area south of the Wissembourg Gap around the Hagenau Forest was the scene of intense fighting in January 1945 as a result of Operation *Nordwind*. When the German offensive was defeated towards the end of January, the Seventh US Army returned north towards the Moder, facing the trace of the Maginot Line. The Wissembourg Gap was a prime objective of Operation *Undertone*, which started on March 15, 1945. The plan was to breach the initial German defensive line along the Moder on

Battle for Steinfeld, March 20–23, 1945

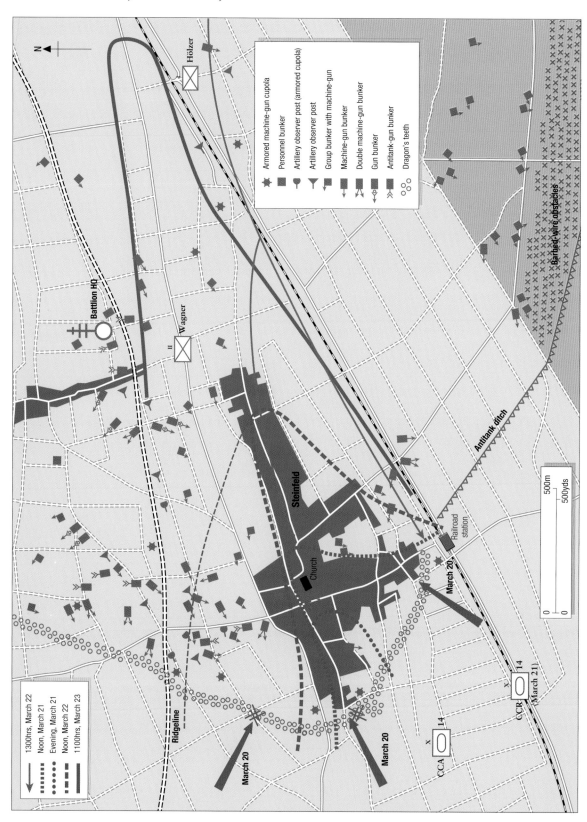

Legend:
- Armored machine-gun cupola
- Personnel bunker
- Artillery observer post (armored cupola)
- Artillery observer post
- Group bunker with machine-gun
- Machine-gun bunker
- Double machine-gun bunker
- Gun bunker
- Antitank-gun bunker
- Dragon's teeth

Hölzer

Wagner

Battlion HQ

Steinfeld

Church

Railroad station

Antitank ditch

Barbed-wire obstacles

Ridgeline

March 20

March 20

March 20

CCA 14

CCR 14 (March 21)

500m
500yds

- 1300hrs, March 22
- Noon, March 21
- Evening, March 21
- Noon, March 22
- 1100hrs, March 23

An infantryman from the 14th Armored Division looks over the trenches outside Steinfeld following the fighting there in late March 1945. Although the commander had intended that the infantry in the town fight from these trenches, in fact they mostly remained in the bunkers during the fighting. (NARA)

a broad front, with the 103rd Division on the left aiming at the Hardt mountains while the 36th Division on the right headed into the Wissembourg Gap. Once the initial German defensive lines along the Maginot Line and above the Moder were overcome, VI Corps planned to inject the 14th Armored Division as its mobile exploitation force, and it was this unit that would eventually become involved in the battle for Steinwald.

As planned, the 36th Division attacked the German defensive line above the Moder near Hagenau in the pre-dawn hours of March 15, and made steady progress into the Hagenau Forest. The German XC Korps gave its units permission to withdraw into the Westwall on Sunday, March 18. By this stage, the 14th Armored Division had been instructed to begin the exploitation phase, and one of its assignments was to break through the Siegfried Line at Steinfeld. This was not a traditional mission according to US Army armored-division tactical doctrine. American armored divisions were very light on infantry, having only three battalions of armored infantry on half-tracks, and attacks on fortified lines ate up infantry at a prodigious rate. However, the corps headquarters decided that the nemy's main resistance had already been broken. The division reached the phase line south of Steinfeld in the early afternoon of Monday, March 19, with Combat Command B (CCB) assigned to the main assault. Artillery strikes were directed against the village of Kapsweyer to the west of the Steinfeld fortified zone at around 1300hrs and fighter-bombers attacked Steinfeld itself around 1430hrs. With a battle brewing, most remaining civilians left the town that evening.

Combat Command B deployed in three task forces, which contained mixed elements from its main components: the 25th Tank Battalion, 68th Armored Infantry Battalion (AIB), and the 125th Armored Engineer Battalion (AEB). The task forces included a company each of tanks and armored infantry supported by a combat-engineer platoon. The division's three armored field-artillery battalions equipped with M7 105mm howitzer motor carriages were all assigned to support the attack. The attacking formation had very

good intelligence on the German fortifications and planned to use the engineer troops to breach the outer cordon of dragon's teeth using high explosives.

The attack began in the pre-dawn hours of March 20 with the engineers using the cover of darkness to place explosive charges on the dragon's teeth west of the town cemetery. The inexperienced garrison in Steinfeld had failed to deploy outposts or patrols to monitor the tank obstacles. A gap was blown through the dragon's teeth, although it later proved to be inadequate for tank passage. The detonations excited the garrison, which began to fire wildly into the obstacle beds. This prevented the American engineers from any further demolition activities to widen the gaps. Around 0630hrs, Task Force Blue, consisting of B/25th Tank Battalion and B/68th AIB, began moving forward out of Kapsweyer. Once clear of the village they came under heavy fire from the Steinfeld defenders but were able to use the hills and terrain features to move closer to the dragon's teeth on the outer perimeter. At noon, the divisional artillery conducted a 15-minute fire mission on the town followed by two minutes of smoke rounds. Two infantry companies, B and C/68th AIB, moved through the dragon's teeth but the wind quickly dispersed the smoke cover. An initial wave of 23 infantrymen reached and occupied the first houses on the west side of Steinfeld, but the remaining infantry was forced to ground by the intense German fire. The tanks remained for the rest of the day providing fire support to the troops trapped in the town. The German defenders remained ensconced in the bunkers and were not aggressive enough to root out the American intruders in the village.

That night, the engineers began moving forward large quantities of high explosive to make three breaches through the dragon's teeth. The attack commenced in the pre-dawn darkness of March 21 with an artillery preparation of 2,500 rounds followed by the demolition of the dragon's teeth, which widened the gaps to about 10ft (3m) wide, enough for the tanks to pass. Combat Command B was reinforced by the division's CCR for the attack, which added much-needed infantry from the 62nd AIB along with the tanks of the 48th Tank Battalion. The infantry attack resumed at 0500hrs; by 0534hrs eight houses had been taken and by 0710hrs the center of the town was in American hands. The troops were extremely surprised to find that many of the innocent-appearing houses were in fact carefully camouflaged pillboxes. Most of the infantry fighting took place in the back yards and alleys of the town since the streets were the main avenue of fire for both the German pillboxes and the American tanks. One of the most dangerous German pillboxes, Stand 234, was camouflaged and could fire up along the main street. The tanks began moving through the dragon's teeth around 1010hrs and additional tank platoons began moving on either side of the town to provide fire against outlying buildings and bunkers. The M4A3 (76mm) tanks found that their gunfire bounced harmlessly off the concrete pillboxes, but that the embrasures could sometimes be silenced.

The western section of the town was the first to be cleared by the US infantry, and by midday the German defenders had suffered about 200 casualties – nearly half their force. The first signs of surrender began to appear as white flags began to pop up here and there. Giesecke briefed the division commander on the situation and suggested that Batallion Weigand in division reserve should be sent into Steinfeld to redeem the situation. Hauptmann Walter Weigand argued otherwise, so the division commander agreed to send Kompanie Hölzer from Weigand's battalion, which was east of the town in the Bienwald woods. A second counterattack force was created from the *Kampfgruppe*'s reserve company, and an improvised attack group was formed from battalion-headquarters troops. At around noont, Panzerkompanie Gekerle with its four tank destroyers arrived in neighboring Vollmersweiler and began shelling American positions on the northern side of the town. Giesecke appointed his adjutant, Hauptmann Werbeck, to take over command in the town after he had to be evacuated to the divisional aid station in the rear; Werbeck would later be awarded the Ritterskreuz (Knight's Cross) for his leadership in the battle.

Kampfgruppe Werbeck launched a counterattack at around 1305hrs, preceded by an artillery barrage on the town to force the American infantry to ground. Kompanie Hölzer attempted to move up from the woods to the railroad station on the southwest side of town via the railroad tracks. A US spotter plane directed artillery fire onto them, which slowed but did not stop their advance. The other force attacked from the eastern side of the town towards the center but was stopped in its tracks by intense American fire. At around 1530hrs 16 US fighter-bombers hit Panzerkompanie Gekerle at the edge of Vollmersweiler, setting several houses ablaze but not knocking out any of the tank destroyers. By evening much of Steinfeld was in American hands. Hölzer's counterattack force around the railroad station had been reduced to half its original strength and was instructed to withdraw towards the eastern end of the town to regroup with the 40 survivors of Werbeck's force; fewer than half a dozen men escaped.

During the night, US engineers created a more efficient breach by bulldozing dirt over the dragon's teeth and using some sections of bridging to create a ramp. The next day's fighting on March 22 got off to a fierce start when an initial 62nd AIB attack in the pre-dawn hours coincided with a German counterattack. At least three US tanks were knocked out by fire from the bunkers. Through the course of the morning US spotter aircraft were able to seal off the town by bringing down artillery fire on further efforts by the

This is one of the 40P8 armored machine-gun cupolas located on the outskirts of Steinfeld. Prior to the fighting it had been entirely encrusted in sod for camouflage, but this has been stripped away by numerous hits from tank fire. (NARA)

German infantry to infiltrate into the town. By 1045hrs the 62nd AIB had reached the eastern side of Steinfeld. The rest of the day was spent clearing out bunkers in the town, and in the afternoon seven M36 90mm tank destroyers and some 155mm guns arrived to help blast the bunkers. By evening the town was firmly in American hands, though there were still pockets of German troops in the bunkers on the southern and eastern fringes. The 905. Volksgrenadier-Division headquarters passed the word to begin a withdrawal at 1900hrs under cover of darkness. By this stage, German casualties totaled about 500 of the original 650 troops that had taken part in the battle, of whom 353 were captured. American casualties in the fighting were under 300 men.

The remnants of Steinwald defense force, renamed Batallion Werbeck, withdrew to the bunkers that guarded the way eastward towards Schaidt. On March 23 Volksgrenadier Regiment 466 began moving into this sector in a futile effort to block the tank advance. Although the pillboxes, *Pantherturme*,

F   UNTERSTAND 230/10, EINHEIT WAGNER, 905. VOLKSGRENADIER-DIVISION, STEINFELD, MARCH 1945

When the Wissembourg Gap was fortified as part of the Westwall in 1938–39, the village of Steinfeld received an especially elaborate treatment, including extensive camouflage efforts to hide the bunkers in the town itself. This particular bunker near the town entrance is a modified version of the Regelbau 10 – Gruppenunderstand mit angehängtem Kampfraum (group bunker with attached combat chamber). This particular type of bunker design was one of the most common in the Westwall, with over 3,000 constructed. It was intended to accommodate a standard squad/section (*Gruppe*) of ten men and also included a fighting compartment (*Kampfraum*) with two machine-gun posts. In the case of the Steinfeld example, the fighting compartment was rearranged by angling the side machine-gun embrasure so that it could

fire down the main street. Besides the two firing positions in the combat compartment, there is a third embrasure on the side of the bunker to cover the two main access doors. This particular bunker has had a false superstructure added above the bunker to make it resemble an ordinary house; several of the bunkers inside Steinfeld received this treatment. In 1944–45 the town's defenses were reinforced by the addition of trench lines and antitank ditches. In addition, a number of pedestal antitank guns and *Pantherturme* were added several miles behind the town along the road to Schaidt to serve as a PaK front. This bunker was held by Einheit Wagner of the 905. Volksgrenadier-Division in March 1945 when the town was attacked by the US Army's 14th Armored Division, as described in the text.

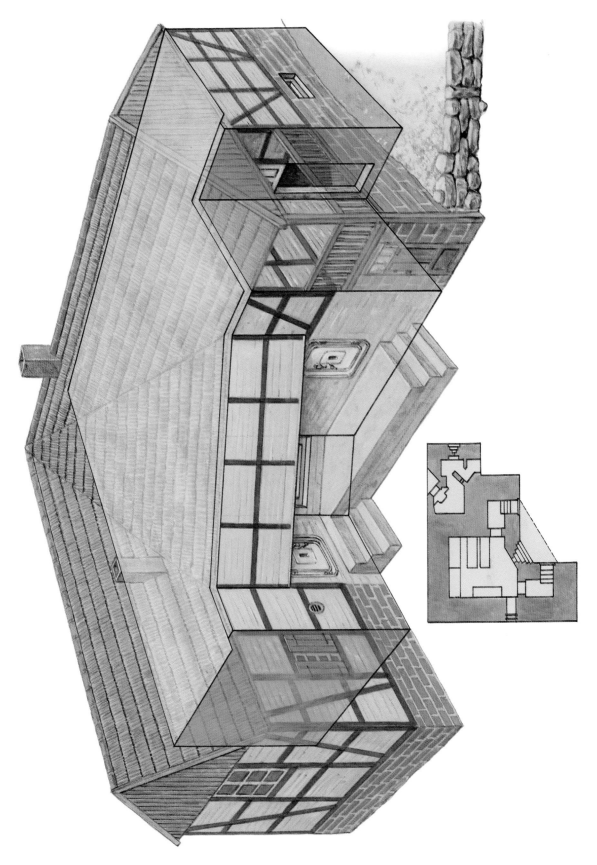

59

and antitank guns along the road to Shaidt slowed the American advance out of Steinfeld, the main defensive belt had been overcome and the momentum of the 14th Armored Division attack picked up. While CCB and CCR were still fighting for Shaidt, CCA had exploited a gap created by the 103rd Division and had reached as far as the Germersheim bridgehead on the Rhine. By this time, the Rhein-Stellung defenses in the Saar-Palatinate had been thoroughly breached all across the front, and AOK 1 was on the verge of a rout.

The battle for Steinfeld provides some idea of the effectiveness of fortifications in the later stages of World War II. This defensive belt was the toughest faced by VI Corps during Operation *Undertone*, and it took three days of fighting to overcome, pitting half of a combat-hardened armored division against a third-rate, under-strength German infantry regiment. Such fortified belts significantly enhanced the defensive capabilities of an increasingly brittle and diminished Wehrmacht. On the other hand, reliance on the fortified sectors and a lack of reserves meant that once the fortification zone was penetrated the defenses were subject to a sudden collapse. Having cleared the Steinfeld Fortification Sector, the 14th Armored Division was able to advance 20 miles (32km) to the Rhine against light opposition in a single day.

Analysis

The West-Stellung was a crutch to help keep the Wehrmacht on its feet after the crippling losses suffered in the summer of 1944. The tenacious defense of the western German frontier in the autumn of 1944 was substantially buttressed by the West-Stellung. Many British and American accounts of the fighting praise German defensive prowess in these campaigns but few recognize the significant role of the West-Stellung. This is in part due to the confusion between the old Westwall, the misnamed Siegfried Line, and the lack of appreciation of the extent of new fortification undertaken under the West-Stellung program. The West-Stellung amplified the original core provided by the Westwall and provided defense in depth. While the Westwall covered about 535 miles (860km) of frontier, the West-Stellung lines were nearly three times as long, stretching for around 1,550 miles (2,500km) with more than 6,000 miles (9,500km) of new trenches. The construction program added about 22,000 new bunkers and gun positions to the remaining 8,000 Westwall bunkers, as well as over 80,000 machine-gun pits and other combat positions. The *Festung* troops added substantial defensive firepower in the form of additional machine guns, antitank guns, and large-caliber artillery.

The value of the West-Stellung declined after the defeat of the Ardennes offensive, due in part to the drastic decline in the combat effectiveness of remaining German formations, but also due to an increasing rigidity in defensive tactics foisted on the Army by Hitler. Führer Directive Nr. 69 of January 21, 1945 demanded that "Any plan to give up a position, a local strongpoint, or a fortress" must be reported directly to him. The West-Stellung contained innumerable miles of unnamed trenches and weapon pits; each and every bunker on the old Westwall had been carefully numbered and Berlin had detailed maps. Retreat from West-Stellung fieldworks attracted little attention in Berlin, but as ludicrous as it sounds, German tactical commanders were obliged to report every time they wished to withdraw from each single Westwall bunker and to report each time a bunker was lost. Failing to do so could result in court martial and summary execution. Hitler's growing fatalism led to the curse of the Westwall: "*Den Westwall halten oder mit dem Westwall untergehen*" ("Hold the Westwall or perish on the Westwall"). The Führer Directive stripped away the German Army's tactical flexibility and substituted it with ominous threats. The directive inadvertently diminished the value of the Westwall bunkers since German commanders quickly learned methods to avoid the consequences. Instead of basing their defenses on the bunkers, they would garrison the pillboxes with as few troops as possible. When the bunkers were quickly overwhelmed or outflanked by Allied attacks, the commanders could honestly report to Berlin that the bunkers had succumbed to the enemy in combat and had not been abandoned. The West-Stellung was the site of the last great defensive battles of the war in the west in March 1945. By the end of the month the Rhine had been comprehensively breached by the Allies along its entire length, as the Wehrmacht was routed in a great *Götterdämmerung*.

THE SITES TODAY

Little of the West-Stellung still exists today except for part of the Westwall. Much of the West-Stellung consisted of fieldworks, which quickly disappeared after the war. Many traces of these still exist, such as the extensive antitank ditches, but there has been little effort to either preserve or catalog the remains. A few bunkers specific to the West-Stellung still exist, including a few Rgl. Nr. 703 PaK bunkers in the Netherlands in the Utrecht area at Buurtsteeg, Juffrouwwijk, Langesteeg, and Leusden. The concrete bunkers of the Westwall were mostly destroyed after the war, but there has been a revival of interest in preserving the few that remain. There are a number of guides to surviving Westwall bunkers, including the book *Der Westwall von Kleve bis Basel* (by Bettinger et al.) listed below; several websites are devoted to the Westwall as well. A number of Westwall sites have been restored as small museums. Several of the Maginot Line forts that were incorporated into the West-Stellung have been preserved as museums, including some of those from the Bitche ensemble such as Fort Simserhof. There are many small traces of the West-Stellung battles; the village of Steinfeld whose capture is detailed here still has an elaborate array of dragon's teeth as well as the remnants of tank traps.

FURTHER READING

This is the first book devoted to the West-Stellung. The massive study of the Westwall by Bettinger and Büren has a chapter devoted to it, as does the excellent study by Groß on the Westwall in the Lower Rhine and Eifel. This account was based on a variety of primary and secondary sources. The US National Archives has a variety of wartime documents, most notably from the Inspekteur der Festungen and General der Pioniere und Festungen in the OKH records; the latter includes extensive records of the OB West Inspekteur der Westbefestigungen and Inspekteur der Landesbefestigungen West offices, as well as many of the subordinate fortification commands. Some of the field-command records, such as those from Heeresgruppen B and G, also have documents dealing with the effort. The US Army's Center for Military History conducted the Foreign Military Studies program after the war to record the experiences of German commanders, and a number of the studies deal directly with the West-Stellung; those listed below are the most relevant but many of the field-army and corps accounts not listed here also have useful details, including maps. The de Beaurepaire report for the French Army

A single *Pantherturm* has survived that was originally deployed with Festung-Pantherturm-Kompanie 1204 near Niederwürzbach in the Hardt mountains in the Saar. After lying derelict for decades, it was recovered and reinstalled at the Westwall museum at Niedersimten. (Neil Short)

provides extensive details on the West-Stellung in the Wissembourg Gap and the Allied campaign against these defenses in March 1945. There are a significant number of books on the Westwall and Maginot Line that touch on the West-Stellung.

US Army Foreign Military Studies

Alberti, Konrad, *Kampfgruppe Alberti and Wehrkreis XII South 15 Mar–28 April 1945* (B-585)

Berg, Kurt, *Wehrkreis XII* (B-060)

Blumentritt, Günther, *Synergy between Mobile Operations and Fixed Fortifications* (B-652)

Bölsen, Hans, *Wehrkreis XII 7–21 March 1945* (B-063)

Botsch, Walter, *Bonn Staff – Remagen Bridge* (B-785)

Eckstein, Walter, *Lower Rhine Fortifications (15 Sep 1943–17 Oct 1944)* (B-834)

——, *Upper Rhine Fortifications (19 Oct 1944–8 Apr 1945)* (B-835)

Eimler, Robert, *Fortress Engineer Commander XXI: September 1944–April 1945* (B-064, B-291)

Fäckenstedt, Ernst, *Wehrkreis VI and Wehrkreis XII Jan 1944–Mar 1945* (B-665)

——, *Wehrkreis XII 22 Mar–11 May 1945* (B-404)

Greiffenberg, Hans, *German Plans for Preventing the Allied Use of Barges and Other River Craft on the Rhine* (P-014)

Höhne, Gustav, *Reconnaissance of the Vosges Positions: 8 Aug–15 Oct 1944* (B-043)

Hossfeld, Walther, *Wehrmacht Commander Karlsruhe 22 Mar–6 May 1945* (B-567)

Janowski, Hermann, *Army Group B Engineer Staff* (B-072)

——, *Obstacle Construction East of the Rhine* (B-105)

Loch, Herbert, *High Command Eifel* (B-065)

Matternklott, Franz, *Wehrkreis VI, 22 Mar–20 Apr 1945* (B-217)

Metz, Richard, *The 15th Army Artillery (March–April 1945)* (B-547)

Schmidt, Hans, *Vosges Defenses* (B-519)

Schramm, Percy, *The German Wehrmacht in the Last Days of the War: 1 January–7 May 1945* (C-020)

Taglichsbeck, Hans, *LXIV Corps Defensive Construction: 16 Sep 1944–25 Feb 1945* (B-504)

Vaterrodt, Franz, *Defense of Strasbourg 1944: 23–25 November 1944* (B-545)

Veiel, Rudolf, *Wehrkreis V, 1 Sep 1943–15 Apr 1945* (B-193)

Wegener, Carl, *Army Group B* (A-695)

Wirtz, Richard, *Army Group B Engineers (1–25 Jan 1945)* (B-172)

——, *Army Group B Engineers and the Remagen Bridgehead* (B-243)

Government studies

Capitaine de Beaurepaire, *À l'assaut de la ligne Siegfried* (French Army: 1948)

Armor in the Attack of Fortified Positions (US Army Armored School: 1950)

Bildheft Neuzeitlicher Stellungsbau (German Army, September 1942, reprinted by Bellona in 1968 as *German Field Works of World War II*)

Breaching the Siegfried Line, XIX Corps, 2 October 1944 (US Army XIX Corps: 1945)

Handbook of the Organisation Todt (MIRS-London: March 1945)

Published accounts

Bettinger, Dieter, et al., *Der Westwall von Kleve bis Basel* (Dörfler: 2002)

Bettinger, Dieter and Büren, Martin, *Der Westwall: Die Geschichte der deutschen Westbefestigungen im Dritten Reich*, 2 vols. (Biblio: 1990)

Christoffel, Edgar, *Krieg am Westwall 1944/45* (Interbook: 1989)

Fuhrmeister, Jörg, *Der Westwall: Geschichte und Gegenwart* (Motorbuch: 2003)

Groß, Manfred, et al., *Der Westwall: Vom Denkmalwert des Unerfreulichen* (Rheinland-Verlag: 1997)

——, *Westwallkämpfe*, (Helios: 2008)

——, *Der Westwall zwischen Niederrhein und Schnee-Eifel* (Rheinland-Verlag: 1982)

Gückelhorn, Wolfgang, *Archäologie des Zweiten Weltkriegs am Mittelrhein* (Helios: Teil I, 2007, Teil 2, 2008)

——, *Das Ende am Rhein: Kriegsende zwischen Remagen und Andernach* (Helios: 2005)

Hansen, Hans-Josef, *Auf den Spuren des Westwalls* (Helios: 2005)

Jentz, Thomas and Doyle, Hilary, *Panther Turrets* (Panzer Tracts: 2005)

——, *Panzer Turrets on Concrete and Wood Stands* (Panzer Tracts: 2004)

Lepage, Jean-Denis, *The Westwall: Siegfried Line 1938–1945* (Nafziger: 2002)

Lippmann, Harry, *Panzersperren und andere Hindernisse* (DAWA: 1987)

Molt, Albert, *Der deutsche Festungsbau von der Memel zum Atlantik 1900–1945* (Dörfler: 1998)

Renn, Walter, *Hitler's West Wall: Strategy in Concrete and Steel 1938–45* (UMI: 1970)

Short, Neil, *Hitler's Siegfried Line* (Sutton: 2002)

——, *Tank Turret Fortifications* (Crowood: 2006)

Threuter, Christina, *Westwall: Bild und Mythos* (Imhof: 2009)

Wetzig, Sonja, *Die deutsche Festungs-Front* (Dörfler: 2004)

INDEX